THIS BOOK WAS DONATED
TO THE HONESTY LIBRARY
AT WESTON FAVELL
SHOPPING CENTRE

FOR YOUR TOMORROW,

WE GAVE OUR TODAY

FOR YOUR TOMORROW,

WE GAVE OUR TODAY

ROBERT FURNESS'S STORY

22554 PRIVATE

"B" COMPANY

6th (S) BATTALION, THE NORTHAMPTONSHIRE REGIMENT

54th INFANTRY BRIGADE

18th DIVISION

By

KENNETH S. BRAWN
(Robert's Great Grandson)

All rights reserved; no part of this publication may be reproduced or transmitted in any form or by any means, electronic or mechanical, including photocopying, recording, or by any information retrieval system without written permission of the Author.

Published by Kenneth S. Brawn
July 2017

Copyright © 2015 Kenneth S. Brawn
ksbrawn@yahoo.co.uk

10 9 8 7 6 5 4 3 2 1

ISBN No. 978-1-5262-0044-0

Kenneth S. Brawn asserts the moral right to be identified as the author of this work.

Although every precaution has been taken in the preparation of this book, and the use of all known copyright obtained, the author assumes no responsibility for errors or omissions. Neither is any liability assumed for damages resulting from the use of the information contained herein.

Other books by Kenneth S. Brawn – Memoirs of an English Cat in Ukraine

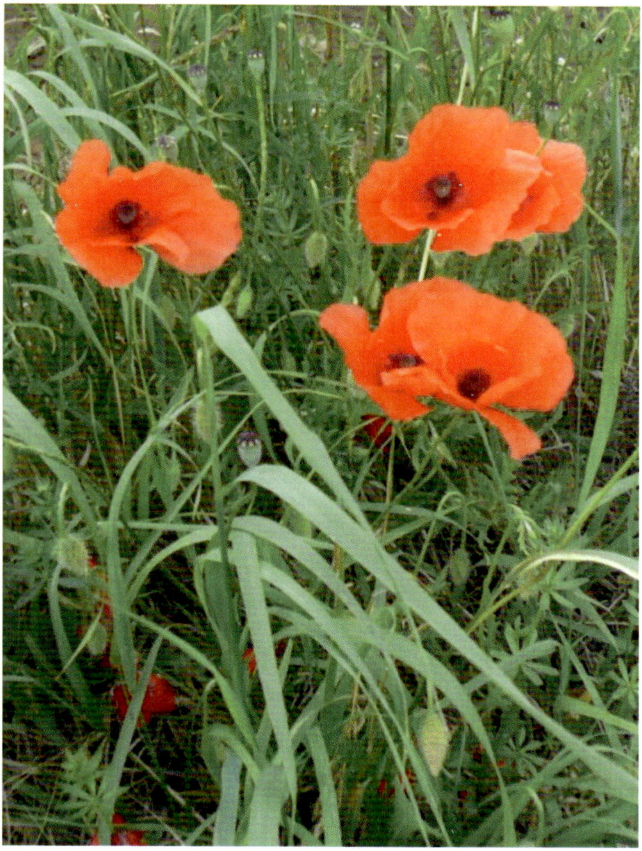

DEDICATED TO
THOSE WHO
HAVE
MADE THE ULTIMATE SACRIFICE
FOR
FREEDOM

AND

THOSE THAT
VOLUNTEERED
TO PUT THEIR LIVES AT RISK
FOR
FREEDOM

AND

THOSE
INNOCENTS
THAT PERISHED AS A CONSEQUENCE OF THE FIGHT
FOR
FREEDOM

6 Million Mobilised

704,803 British Combatants Died

THEY SHALL GROW NOT OLD

They shall grow not old, as we that are left grow old:

Age shall not weary them, nor the years condemn.

At the going down of the sun and in the morning

WE WILL REMEMBER THEM

From Laurence Binyon's poem *For the Fallen*, September 1914

Through this book, my descendants are requested to keep our lineage alive in memory

WE MUST REMEMBER THEM

ROBERT FURNESS

AWARDED - BRITISH WAR MEDAL & VICTORY MEDAL
MEDALS & RETURNED EFFECTS

MEMORIAL PLAQUE

THANKS

WHEN YOU GO HOME, TELL THEM OF US AND SAY
FOR YOUR TOMORROW, WE GAVE OUR TODAY

John Maxwell Edmonds (21 January 1875 – 18 March 1958)

First and foremost, I need to posthumously thank Robert and his loving wife Gertrude who, through their positive contribution to life, made it possible for me to pen this tribute.

Sincere thanks go to Sharon Brawn (née Tulej), mother of Robert's great, great grandchildren, Robert's grandson David Smart and my 3rd cousin Paul Furness for their full support. As you will read later, help also came from a surprise source in Stuart and Iris May Gooch (née Furness), Robert's great grandson and granddaughter respectively; they have safely kept Robert's medals and effects over the years.

I must also thank Jon-Paul Carr for his unreserved help and direction with the technical aspects of my research.

The aforementioned unselfishly provided their detailed research into the Furness and Smart family trees and the 6th (Service) Battalion, The Northamptonshire Regiment. This gave me direction and saved me a huge amount of time and effort. Through their full cooperation, we solved many unanswered questions and reconnected Robert's medals and effects with his life story – although I say it myself, this is a fantastic achievement by all concerned.

The majority of the book is based on the 6th (Service) Battalion, The Northamptonshire Regiment War Diary (WO-95-2044-2_1 and WO-95-2044-2_2) plus additional information gleaned from the 18th Division, Trench Mortar Battery War Diary (WO-95-2026-1_1 and WO-95-2026-1_2).

The above Diaries are from the National Archives (http://www.nationalarchives.gov.uk/) and to quote them, *"these records are the unit war diaries of the British Army in the First World War. They are not personal diaries (try the Imperial War Museum or Local Record Offices for those). They are part of a large series of records, WO 95, which contains many more diaries scheduled for digitisation."*

Thanks also go to:

1. Rushden Research Group - http://www.rushdenheritage.co.uk/main-index.html,
2. The Royal British Legion - http://www.britishlegion.org.uk/,
3. The Commonwealth War Graves commission - http://www.cwgc.org/,
4. The Imperial War Museum - http://www.iwm.org.uk/visits/iwm-london,
5. Forces War Records - https://www.forces-war-records.co.uk/ ,
6. Ancestry - http://home.ancestry.co.uk/,
7. The Great War 1914-1918 - http://www.greatwar.co.uk/

My research took me to the Somme battlefields on numerous occasions where I visited the following, must-see, Museums:

1. Avril Willaim's Guest House Museum - http://www.avrilwilliams.eu/
2. Thiepval Visitor centre - http://www.somme-battlefields.com/memory-place/thiepval-memorial-and-visitor-centre,
3. Musée Somme 1916 - Albert - http://www.musee-somme-1916.eu/index.php?lang=en,
4. Pérrone Historial - http://www.somme-battlefields.com/memory-place/peronne-historial-museum-great-war

Thanks also go to the following gentlemen who took the time to record their experiences with the Imperial War Museum:

1. Morris, Ross Charles (IWM interview), (sound) Made by: IWM (Production company) 1992-05-12 12569
2. Collins, Frederick E (IWM interview), (sound) Made by: IWM (Production company) 1984 8229
3. Holmes, Frederick William Henry (IWM interview), (sound) Made by: IWM (Production company) 1985 9147

I wish to point out that a great deal of the cleaned information overlapped and/or duplicated other sources of information. With the exception of identified sources, the National Archive material (Crown Copyright) and because non-Crown Copyright duration has lapsed, specific reference / copyright allocation to specific sources is not considered appropriate, or in fact, possible.

I do, however, thank again the splendid work of the above organisations and dedicated people, because, without them, this story would have been lost forever.

INTRODUCTION

100 YEARS
TO THE MINUTE LATER
I WALKED IN HIS FOOTSTEPS
AND
JOINED HIM IN BATTLE

As a young child, my mother, Mary Brawn (née Smart**),** once mentioned an ancestor who had died in World War One but as far as I can remember, that's as far as the conversation went. In my very early teens and not finding a "Brawn" on Irchester's War Memorial, this individual worked himself to the back of my mind.

Over the years and even knowing the Brawn name wasn't there, I was always drawn back to the Memorial to repeat the search but as you already know, my ancestor remained hidden in plain sight. It's as if I wasn't supposed to find him until the time was right.

Through life's twists and turns, the thought of this person kept returning but being a travelling man, time, connections, location, circumstance and stimulus were never right for me to glean the details; that is, until my 63rd birthday when everything just came together.

The book is a transcription of the 6th (Service) Battalion, The Northamptonshire Regiment's War Diary. The Diary's hand written content is presented in *Bold Bradley Hand ITC font* and the typed content is presented in this standard Calibri font. The War Diary transcription is delivered, as far as possible, in full, as presented, as written with associated colouring and including all mistakes. A few maps have been left out or revised slightly to provide focus and the Diary appendices have been repositioned to provide continuity.

As we get into the War Diary, I've drawn on my brother Kevin's and my military experiences and I've put myself in Robert's shoes and as such, I've tried to express what I think Robert may have felt and thought.

Robert tells his story in this Times New Roman font and his *"thoughts" are presented in Italics*. To aid the reader; omissions and / or inserted text **is presented in** grey.

Throughout the book I've identified Irchester men who died during the war up to the point of Robert's death and I've used narrative license to allow Robert to "remember them" at the appropriate point in time. I need to point out that due to the constraints of war, Robert would not have known of the deaths so quickly, if at all.

To try and give you some perspective of the fear and grief the families, Irchester village and Battalions may have experienced, I've presented those who perished in chronological date of death – significant dates and names are in red.

24-08-14	West, Harry, Lance-Corporal, 8304, 1st Battalion (B Company) 1st Norfolk Regiment
15-10-14	Watts, Alfred George Bertram, Boy 1st Class, J/23432, HMS Hawke, Royal Navy
13-11-14	Wildman, Percy Thomas, Private, 3/10009, 1st Battalion Northamptonshire Regiment
13-11-14	White, John, Private, 9613, 1st Battalion Northamptonshire Regiment
21-12-14	James, Alfred, Private, 9842, 1st Battalion Northamptonshire Regiment
11-03-15	Bayes, Horace, Private, 14377, 2nd Battalion Northamptonshire Regiment
12-03-15	Neale, Alan, Private, (Number unknown), 1st Battalion Northamptonshire Regiment
09-05-15	Atthews, Joseph John, Private, 12779, 1st Battalion Northamptonshire Regiment
09-05-15	Bayes, Joseph, Private, 3/10350, 1st Battalion Northamptonshire Regiment
09-05-15	Richardson, William, Private, 3/9899, 2nd Battalion Northamptonshire Regiment
09-05-15	Clements, George, Private, 12805, 2nd Battalion Northamptonshire Regiment
28-08-15	King, Frederick, Private, 9650, 1st Battalion Northamptonshire Regiment
25-09-15	Whiteman, Sidney, Private, 3910, 1/4th Battalion Northamptonshire Regiment
25-09-15	Cartwright, Alfred, Private, 3/10288, 1st Battalion Northamptonshire Regiment
27-09-15	George, Ernest (Titus), Private, 15292, 7th Battalion Northamptonshire Regiment
12-10-15	Norman, Walter James, Private, 16886, 1st Battalion Northamptonshire Regiment
26-11-15	Brudenell, Frederick, Private, 17617, 6th Battalion, Northamptonshire Regiment
05-06-16	Shrives, Herbert, Private, 23051, 3rd Battalion Northamptonshire Regiment
08-07-16	Atthews, Frederick Jonathan, Private, 12469, 2nd Battalion Northamptonshire Regiment
23-07-16	Reynolds, William Charles, Private, 17598, 1st Battalion Northamptonshire Regiment
17-08-16	Freeman, Arthur, Private, 23838, 1st Battalion Northamptonshire Regiment
20-08-16	Partridge, Frederick, Private, 8976, 1st Battalion Northamptonshire Regiment
03-09-16	Joyce, William, Private, 2166, 9th Battalion East Surrey Regiment
26-09-16	Magee, Malcolm William, Private, 15907, 6th Battalion Northamptonshire Regiment
01-10-16	Percival, Raymond Alexander, Private, 23857, 1st Battalion Northamptonshire Regiment
27-10-16	George, Leonard, Private, 18106, 2nd Battalion Northamptonshire Regiment
13-11-16	Sears, Joseph, Private Arthur, 22976, 4th Battalion Bedfordshire Regiment
17-02-17	Jeffries, John F, Private, 18147, 6th Battalion Northamptonshire Regiment

18-02-17	Luck, Fred, Lance-Corporal, 18142, 6th Battalion Northamptonshire Regiment
11-03-17	Needham, William Mackness, Private, 40070, 7th Battalion Northamptonshire Regiment
20-03-17	Percival, John, Private, 31009, 6th Battalion Northamptonshire Regiment
09-04-17	Clark, Albert, Private, 5795, 11th Battalion Suffolk Regiment
09-04-17	George, Jesse, Rifleman, 474116, 1st/12th Battalion London Regiment (The Rangers)
09-04-17	Sawford, John, Private, 28016, 1st Battalion East Yorkshire Regiment
26-04-17	Laughton, Harry Conyers, Private, 202248, 1st/4th Battalion Yorkshire Regiment
03-05-17	Furness, Robert, Private, 22554, 6th Bn. "B" Coy, Northamptonshire Regiment

To also provide understanding, the British Army is generally structured as follows:

Type of Unit	Contains	Personnel	Commanded by
Section		8 - 10	Corporal
Platoon	3 Sections	30	Captain, Lieutenant or 2nd Lieutenant
Company (Coy)	3 Platoons	100	Major
Battalion / Regiment	5 - 7 Companies	550 - 750	Lieutenant Colonel
Brigade	3 - 5 Battalions	5,000	Brigadier
Division	2 - 3 Brigades	10,000	Major General

Now that you have a flavour, you are cordially invited to turn the page to experience Robert's life and my journey through a space / time wormhole...

Table of Contents

100 YEARS	1
PEACE AND FREEDOM	2
LIFE STARTS TO DISINTEGRATE	5
REALITY HITS HOME	8
WORLD WAR ONE	9
NO CHOICE	15
DECISION MADE	18
THE FRONT	21
BATTLE OF THE SOMME 1 JULY – 18 NOVEMBER 1916	30
THE BATTLE OF ALBERT	31
THE BATTLE OF BAZENTIN RIDGE AND CAPTURE OF TRONES WOOD	59
THE BATTLE OF THIEPVAL RIDGE	91
THE BATTLE OF THE ANCRE HEIGHTS	123
THE BATTLE OF THE ANCRE	131
OPERATIONS ON THE ANCRE	139
THE GERMAN RETREAT TO THE HINDENBURG LINE	154
THE THIRD BATTLE OF THE SCARPE	168
RESTING WITH MY MATES	173
FINAL JOURNEY	174
THE CONNECTION	176
AT PEACE	179
IN MY FOOTSTEPS	180
CONCENTRATION OF GRAVES - BURIAL RETURNS DOCUMENT	187
KEN, IN REFLECTION	188
OTHER FAMILY MEMBERS RECOGNISED	191
INNOCENT FAMILY VICTIMS OF WORLD WAR TWO	195
ABOUT THE AUTHOR	197
THE SOLDIER	200
IN FLANDERS FIELD	201
HISTORY OF THE POPPY EMBLEM	202
ORIGINS OF THE TWO MINUTES PAUSE	209

100 YEARS

I'VE BEEN DEAD
FOR 100 YEARS.
WHEN I SAY DEAD,
I MEAN,
IN BODY AND MEMORY

Unlike the fine weather of the 3rd May 1917, it's a cold and wet 3rd May 2017 as some of my great grandchildren visit my grave.

Stuart Gooch   Ken, 2nd from right & his siblings

I'm deeply moved by their and other family members efforts in the laying of wreaths of remembrance of my sacrifice but looking down at them in their moment of reflection, I can feel that they want to understand why I left my loving Trudy and family knowing that my chances of returning were small and also, what happened in the war, how did I die and where?

Well, here's my story and the answers…

PEACE AND FREEDOM

Ten years before the end of the Victorian era, England had been in the grip of a heat wave for four days with average temperatures being over 80°F.

In a little cottage[1] in the Northamptonshire hamlet of Astcote, my lace maker mother Ann, must have been extremely uncomfortable when she delivered me on Friday the 8th July 1881 to a free world at relative peace.

I'm quite sure my brothers, eight year old George Edward and six year old William George were quite happy with me because we remained very close throughout our lives.

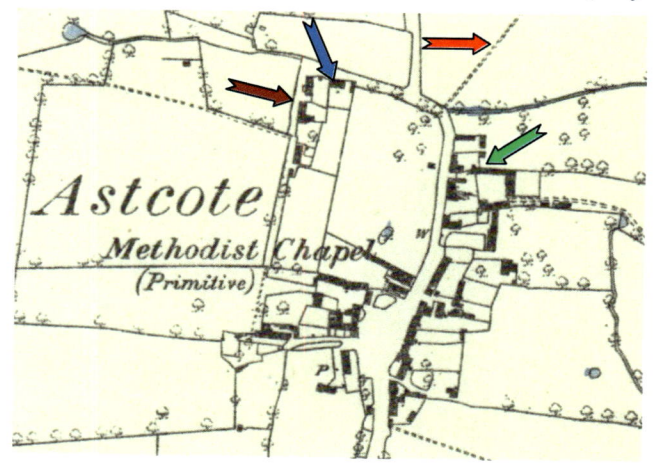

As with all women, I can only imagine that our lodger, 22 year old Elizabeth Jones, being three years younger than my mother, cheerfully

---

[1] The 1881 Census has 26 pages. It shows the Recorder started South of Astcote and travelled in an easterly anticlockwise direction towards the Folly and up to Dalscote before entering Eastcote. The previous entry before Astcote is The Boot public house in the lower end of Eastcote. It makes sense that the Recorder would have taken the shortest route to Astcote, this being the footpath (red arrow) from The Boot.

The Census has the shoe factory and beer house (green arrow and now Shoe Maker Close) recorded at the end of his route on page 26. Astcote census starts on page 13 and on page 15, 10th entry (No. 85), has Ann Turnifs in a cottage two doors away from her parents, Edward and Sarah Ann Pell. This would indicate that the Recorder has continued on his anticlockwise direction along what is now known as Sutton's Walk.

I discovered from the resident that their house (dark blue arrow) used to be three one up / one down "cottages". The house next to it on the left and on the corner is number 7. It is my belief that Robert was born in one of the cottages in Sutton's Walk and most probably one of the two identified by the brown arrow.

shared the load of the new arrival. My brother, John Henry followed me into the world in October 1883.

Life in the agricultural environment was as normal as it could be in a hamlet of about 120 people and most of our time, when not attending school, was taken up with helping mum and playing in the fields.

On the 25th November 1890, the mild, unsettled weather changed dramatically with temperatures plummeting and snow falling. Mum hadn't been well for a while and she was spending more and more time between the Workhouse Infirmary and bed. Four days later, on Saturday the 29th November, at the age of nine, my life was shattered when George told us that mum had gone to heaven and she couldn't come back to look after us anymore. I was to learn later that mum had died from a disease called [2]Dropsy.

My world just fell apart over the next few days. Many people came and went with George finally telling us that because there was little money to go around and we were too young to provide for our own keep, there was no other option but for William, Henry and I to be placed in the Towcester Workhouse while he, being seventeen and already in work, was to live with our grandparents, Edward and Sarah Ann Pell.

Life was turned on its head but we followed George's instructions and by knuckling down, looking after each other and following orders and routines, we came out the other end, stronger for the ordeal. George, whenever he could, kept in touch and provided what little he could spare.

It wasn't easy but life's purpose and rhythm returned and in my middle teens, school was replaced with work in the fields. As young men do, I moved around to find more meaningful and better paid work and in the latter part of the 1890's, while working as an engine driver in the local water works, I met a beautiful shoe lift maker called Gertrude Frances Stokes.

Love led to Trudy and I getting married, in extremely cold and severe frosty weather, in the Wellingborough Register Office on the

---

[2] **Modern term – Oedema** - a condition characterized by an excess of watery fluid collecting in the cavities or tissues of the body

24th December 1900 and we lived happily, just up the road from my brother George, on the new estate in Rushden Road, Wymington.

1901 saw me move into the boot and shoe trade to be near Trudy and we moved to 12 Upton Place Rushden. Here, after a week of reasonably fine weather and temperatures around 80°F, we were blessed with the birth of Alfred Robert on the 24th August 1901. We were further rewarded when Annie was born, on a fine day of above average temperature, on the 5th February 1903.

Just over three years later, on a cool 65°F, dry but sunny 13th July 1906, Trudy gave birth to Lucy Jane at our new home of 13 Albion Place Rushden. Life wasn't easy but we got by and I remember the good times of long walks and playing with the kids on Sundays; life had sense, purpose and rhythm.

Another move took us to 13 Greens Yard Rushden where, during a very unsettled month, our beautiful Lily was born on the 29th March 1908.

In 1910 everybody was talking about the sighting of Halley's Comet as being a bad omen and this seemed to come true when, to everybody's great sadness, a very sickly Eric was born on the 27th October; our mood reflected the dull and cold weather. At this time Trudy was doing shoe work from home which helped with income and being around to look after the children, especially poor Eric.

Despite Eric's difficulties, life was full of hope and as we had no inkling of the troubles that were brewing in Eastern Europe, or those that would quickly shake our own family to the core, the sense, purpose and rhythm remained and we were at peace with the world.

LIFE STARTS TO DISINTEGRATE

Our first heartache was the death of Eric on the 2nd September 1911. We tried everything to help the poor child but after 9 months of fighting the wasting disease, I like to believe that he decided that the warm and sunny day was the right time for us to part. Trudy and I were beside ourselves and although words failed us, everybody accepted that his passing was a blessing for all concerned; I will never forget his little grave.

After a while, sense, purpose and rhythm returned and in 1913 we took the opportunity to move to 6 Fish's Terrace, Townwell Lane, Irchester.

It was here, on a very warm and pleasant 28th June 1914, we heard of the assassination, in Sarajevo, of Austrian Archduke Franz Ferdinand at the hands of a Gavrilo Princip. Apparently, he was a Serbian nationalist with ties to a secretive military group known as the Black Hand but this didn't really mean much to us. Trudy was heavily pregnant again and pushing the news of the Archduke to one side, the rhythm continued and our hopes for the future remained high.

July 1914 started off with high temperatures around 89°F but it became a little more bearable when nearly half an inch of rain fell on the 3rd.

The *Rushden Echo* reported on the 5th that the German Kaiser promised Austria *"the full support of Germany"* if they decided to take action against Serbia. With the continuing pleasure of the warm weather, the news didn't really bother us because these events were far away and there was no way they would affect us.

Although the weather was cooling, our spirits were lifted higher with the birth of Phyllis May on my birthday of the 8th July and the festivities continued with Lucy Jane's birthday on the 13th. However, these joyous occasions were soon overshadowed by the announcement, on the 14th, that the Austro-Hungarian Ministers had decided that action was to be taken against Serbia; again, we had no idea how this could affect us so we just shrugged it off.

The atmosphere in the Country seemed to follow the cooler, cloudy and more changeable weather when, on the 19th July, the Council of Austro-

Hungarian Ministers approved a draft ultimatum which they presented to Serbia on the 23rd. Apparently, the ultimatum said the Serbs had 48 hours to agree to an Austro-Hungarian inquiry into the Archduke's assassination, that Serbia must suppress all anti-Austrian propaganda and they were to also, within its borders, take steps to root out and eliminate terrorist organisations, especially the Black Hand.

The following day, the *Rushden Echo* reported that the German Government had submitted a note to the Entente Governments of Britain, France and Russia, saying that they approved the Austrian ultimatum. The report also stated that this action had triggered the British Foreign Minister, Sir Edward Grey, to initiate proposals for an international conference in order to avert war; this was the first time that we began to think, perhaps, life was about to change.

In the meantime, the *Rushden Echo* reported that the Belgian Government had declared that, in the event of war, Belgium would uphold her neutrality *"whatever the consequences"*.

The next day, the 25th, it was reported that the Serbian Government had ordered Mobilisation, Austria-Hungary had severed diplomatic relations with Serbia, the Austro-Hungarian Minister had left Belgrade and the Serbian Government had started to move from Belgrade to Nish. Although diplomatic relations were deteriorating, our rhythm of life remained and again, we just shrugged it off.

We read on the 26th July that the Austro-Hungarian Government had ordered Partial Mobilisation against Serbia, the Montenegrin Government had ordered Mobilisation, the British Admiralty countermanded orders for dispersal of the Fleets and the Kaiser had returned from the Baltic to Berlin.

People's moods reflected the breezy weather, when, on the 28th, Austria-Hungary declared war on Serbia, the German Government rejected British proposals for the international conference and the British Fleets were ordered to a war footing.

The breezy weather continued into the 29th which saw the Russian Government order Partial Mobilisation on the borders of Austria-Hungary. In the evening, the Russian Minister for War, without the knowledge of the

Tsar, ordered General Mobilisation and Belgrade was bombarded by Austrian artillery. The German Government then made proposals to secure British neutrality just as the British Admiralty sent a warning telegram to the Fleets and the British War Office sent out telegrams ordering a "*Precautionary Period*"; world events were changing and changing fast.

REALITY HITS HOME

On the 30th July, the Russian Tsar signed the order for Mobilisation of the Russian Army and what was more important, the British Government rejected Germany's proposals for British neutrality. Life's rhythm took a little knock after we understood that this move was effectively declaring war on Germany if they moved against British Allies.

From this point, the news just got worse. The 31st saw the Belgians, Russians, Austro-Hungarian and Turkish Governments order General Mobilisation, the German Government sent an ultimatum to Russia while declaring a state of *"threat of war"* and here, in Britain, the London Stock Exchange was closed. Although none of this affected us directly, life's rhythm was being disturbed and the future didn't look so rosy.

As with the cool and unsettled weather, we entered a topsy-turvy few days where it was reported that the British Government had mobilised the Royal Navy and guaranteed naval protection to the French but then, on the 2nd August, the British Government proclaimed a moratorium, only to then guarantee support to Belgium. Then, the very next day, the 3rd, they issued an order for General Mobilisation and the requisition of shipping. During all of this, and effectively sealing a British declaration of war, Germany declared war on France.

Talking to George and others at work, we all agreed that what was happening didn't look good but because we had no idea of what happens when war is declared, we just took it in our stride and, with a small sense of unease in the back of our minds, the sense, purpose and rhythm of life continued.

When Germany crossed into Belgium and attacked Liège, life, like newspaper consumption, began to run at fever pitch. On the morning of the 5th August we awoke to the news that the British ultimatum requesting Germany to withdraw had been ignored and that the official British declaration of war had been issued. The consequences of this declaration still didn't sink in and little did we realise that the first few years of our little Phyllis May's life, not that she would know or understand, were destined to be governed by World War One.

WORLD WAR ONE

The 5th August was a miserable day with the temperature dropping to 65°F and nearly an inch of rain falling while everybody was saying, *"It'll all be over by Christmas"*; this, in itself, gave hope. We also didn't have any concept of what war entailed or how far it would involve us so we just went to work with this growing unease that the rhythm of life was going to be drastically altered.

We kept reading the *Rushden Echo* with disbelief – Montenegro had declared war on Austria-Hungary, we had sunk the German minelayer *"Königin Luise"* because it had been laying mines off Southwold and the first meeting of the British War Council had been held.

On the 6th, Austria-Hungary declared war on Russia, the Serbs declared war on Germany and the Battle of the Frontiers began in France.

It was reported that Lord Kitchener had replaced Herbert Asquith as the Secretary of State for War, *"H.M.S. Amphion"* had been sunk off Yarmouth by one of the German mines and *"H.M.S. Bristol"* had been in action against the *"Karlsruhe"* in the West Indies.

Unease was steadily growing in my mind when, on the 7th, it was reported that the city of Liège had been occupied by the Germans, the first units of the British Expeditionary Force had landed in France, French troops had crossed the Alsace frontier into the lands east of the River Rhine and *"H.M.S. Gloucester"* had been in action against the German ships *"Goeben"* and *"Breslau"* off the coast of Greece. In discussion, George and I just couldn't understand how things could move so fast.

The 8th August saw Montenegro sever diplomatic relations with Germany, the Battle of Mulhouse started, the Swiss ordered Mobilisation, British forces crossed the frontier into Togoland to occupy Lome and *"H.M.S. Astraea"* had bombarded Dar es Salaam. Our rhythm of life became even more unsettled as the bad news kept coming and as a consequence, more effort was being put into talking than working.

On the 9th August, it was reported that *"H.M.S. Birmingham"* had sank the German submarine *"U-15"* in the North Sea.

With the continuous deluge of bad news, we unconsciously questioned the sense, purpose and rhythm of life and our unease turned to apprehension as it began to dawn on us that our future was changing forever.

The first two weeks of August were truly hard to comprehend - the faster the developments, the faster the heartbeat, the faster the heartbeat, the faster the developments. The weather improved during the second week with temperatures reaching 80°F but this did little to cheer us up or calm our nerves.

We read that France had attacked Germany, only to lose and sustain 329,000 casualties to Germany's 256,000 and the Battle of Mons, Marne and Ypres returned another 760,000 casualties; the numbers just kept growing and were beyond belief.

The *Rushden Echo* reported on the 21st August that a meeting of the Recruiting Committee of the Northants Territorial Force Association had stated that they were anxious to recruit 100,000 men for Lord Kitchener's Army. The meeting said that these numbers were needed just until the end of the war but if the war lasted more than three years, individuals could leave or re-enlist. Suddenly the, *"it'll all be over by Christmas"*, was in real doubt.

The village mood also took a knock with the report, on the 24th August, of the first village war related death of Harry West, number 8304, a Lance-Corporal of B Company of the 1st Battalion, The 1st Norfolk Regiment; the war had penetrated the village heart.

On the 28th August, we read that the Royal Navy had sunk 3 German cruisers during the North Sea Battle of Heligoland Bight but *"HMS Pathfinder"* had been torpedoed and lost. On the Eastern Front, it was reported that Russia had failed in its attack on Prussia who had captured 90,000 prisoners. Worse was to come in that, on their second attempt, Russia again lost, racking up another 320,000 casualties.

While this was going on, Serbia beat Austria-Hungary, the Ottoman Empire attacked Russia at Odessa and Sevastopol and Britain, with France, were fighting against Germany in South West Africa, Togoland, Cameroon and German and British East Africa. The world just seemed to be on fire in places that we hadn't even heard of.

On the 4th September, the *Rushden Echo* reported that 1,555 men had enlisted in Northamptonshire, more recruits were leaving virtually every day and on the 11th September, a further 279 recruits had volunteered. Subconsciously, developments were becoming embedded in my mind but because of my age, my sense of purpose in life was still heavily weighted in favour of Trudy and the children.

With autumn arriving towards the end of September, the weather started to turn colder. The chill was keenly felt with the second report of a war death of another villager on the 5th October, Alfred Watts, Boy 1st Class, number J/23432 of HMS Hawke, Royal Navy; what made it worse was that he was just a boy, literally, with his whole life ahead of him.

The sense, purpose and rhythm of life was helped with the Harvest Festival, Halloween and Guy Fawkes' Night celebrations bringing family, friends and communities together but as the embers of Guy Fawkes' Night turned cold, we read that Japan had joined Britain and attacked China at Tsingtao on the 7th November. This confused my brother George and me; we just couldn't understand why Japan would need to get involved because they were on the other side of the world and they hadn't been attacked.

Further down the page we read that the Pacific Islands of German New Guinea and Samoa had surrendered to Australia and New Zealand and with this, we decided that this war, "*that will be over by Christmas*" had just become a truly global war that wouldn't be over by Christmas. That said, we then decided that it wasn't a truly global war, as yet, because America was staying neutral.

Double tragedy struck on the 13th November with the report of the deaths of Percy Wildman, number 3/10009 and John White, number 9613, both Privates of the 1st Battalion, The Northamptonshire Regiment; two deaths on the same day and from the same Battalion subdued talk amongst the old men frequenting the village seat.

The next thing we learned was that, on the 8th December, Britain had defeated the German Navy in the South Atlantic Battle of the Falklands but we had lost two cruisers with all hands.

Christmas preparations were shattered and morale was hit very hard on the 16th December when the German Navy raided the East Coast towns of Whitby, Scarborough and Hartlepool leaving 137 dead and 592 wounded. This was totally devastating and it left its mark on the population with many people questioning the meaning and celebration of Christmas. Outrage was levelled, and rightly so, at the German Navy for attacking civilians and at the Royal Navy for not stopping them. The war, which we hadn't started or wanted to get involved in, had penetrated British living rooms.

Alfred James, Private, number 9842 of the 1st Battalion, The Northamptonshire Regiment was reported killed on the 21st December and although it still affected us, living in a small village and being who we are, parents with loved children, we couldn't let the kids Christmas be spoilt by, as we said to them, "*a silly little war*", so on the 25th we gathered under the tinsel and paper decorations with brother George, his wife Kate and their 10 kids and after a prayer for those taking part in the War, we had lashings and lashings of goose and fun.

Little did we know it but at that very same moment the Christmas spirit was being shared on the Western Front where certain sections of the British and German trenches laid down their guns, exchanged gifts, sang carols and played football in no-man's land. A few days later, the newspaper report of this event gave us a sign and hope that the end may be in sight but as we continued reading we just couldn't comprehend that the very next day, those very same men started killing each other again; it just beggared belief.

Christmas came and went, the number of casualties kept rising and talk had changed from, "*it'll be all over by Christmas*" to, "*when will it end?*" The war was only 5 months old and one million men had died – we just couldn't believe the numbers that were being published. We could only sit back and morbidly read the developments and the regular casualty lists. It was difficult to read the *Rushden Echo* because it kept feeding my dilemma but read I did.

The 29th January 1915 edition reported that the Labour Exchange would be formally used as the recruitment office for all branches of His Majesty's service.

More casualties were reported over the coming months:

        Private H Bayes   11th March 1915
        Private A Neal   12th March 1915

On the 2nd April, the *Rushden Echo* told the story of an underage lad who borrowed a pair of long trousers to replace his shorts so that he could, and did, successfully join up. It went on to say that he was saved because his friends telephoned the authorities.

During this period, our beautiful Lucy Jane was taken very ill and she finally succumbed to Pneumonia on the 3rd April; poor, poor child. She was sweet, innocent and full of fun and only 8 years old and her passing mortified the family – her death was not like those on the Western Front, her death was real.

The *Rushden Echo* reported on the 9th that the 5th Gordon's and returning soldiers who were on leave were visiting Rushden to stimulate recruiting; this, and older folk's talk, fuelled my dilemma.

My anxiety wasn't helped with the terrible news of the Germans use of chlorine gas at the Battles of Ypres and Gallipoli. Death was all around and all I could think of was, *Why?! Why?! Why?! What's happening to mankind?! What have we done to deserve this?! Where do I fit into all of this?! I'm 32, I have a wife and 4 children, where do I fit in?! What must I do?!*

The 25th April saw the *Rushden Echo* reporting that the Australians and New Zealanders had attacked Gallipoli but the news of the attack was overshadowed by reports that the Turks had taken up to one and a half million Armenian men, women and children into the desert and left them there to die. We just couldn't comprehend why human beings could do such things; *why?!*

I was relieved to read the April reports that the Germans had changed their focus towards the Eastern front with Russia and this had reduced the action on the Western Front. I asked myself, *what's happening to us when we feel relieved to hear that a country has moved its killing front away from us and towards another country? It's not right but I just don't feel ashamed of my feelings.*

The 5th May was an even darker day when news came in that the Germans had torpedoed the civilian ship "*Lusitania*" and 1,198 civilians had lost their lives; again, I asked myself, *why is this madness happening?*

NO CHOICE

Life's sense of purpose and rhythm had disintegrated, uncertainty occupied the air and decisions became more complicated. I ask you, how do you plan for tomorrow when you have no idea what today will bring? The only thing that kept us stable was family life but this, in itself, was a double edged sword. Children's innocence and happiness with life's little things allowed me to break away but after the joy, reality returned all too quickly.

The *Rushden Echo* regularly kept us informed and as time progressed the pressure to take the King's Shilling was ratcheted up to the point of blackmail. The thought in the back of every male mind was, *if I don't volunteer, I will be called a coward and my family will live in shame.* Female thoughts were, *he feels he's compelled to go because he doesn't want shame to fall on us. I don't want him to go but I must be seen to be strong and supportive in his decision to join the fight.*

Everybody was talking about it, it was there, always, the pressure. In deep thought over a cup of tea, it suddenly hit my stomach...

THERE IS NO CHOICE!

Unintentionally, newspapers kept the pressure on through their reporting and casualty lists. Reports of the 9th May hit hard when it was reported that four lads from the village, all Privates, had perished - Joseph John Atthews, William Richardson, who was only 17, Joseph Bays and George Clements; we heard that it was probably in the Second Battle of Ypres.

Italy joined the war on the British side on the 23rd June and I asked myself, *if they are joining after nearly a year of war, what needs to happen for this to end and what will the end be like?* It was truly frightening and it wasn't helped with the *Rushden Echo*'s 21st August report that another village lad, Private Fred King, had been killed.

The casualty lists and village sorrow continued with the deaths of Privates Alfred Cartwright and Sidney Whiteman on the 25th September, this being closely followed by Private Ernest George on the 27th. So many deaths coming so quickly gave rise to sickening and conflicting feelings towards my family – *I don't want to leave Trudy and the kids but I should go and finish the battle that the lads have paid the ultimate price for – they must not have died in vain.*

On the 30th September, the *Rushden Echo* showed photos of recruits about to leave with headings such as, "*the Men Who Point the Way to Duty's call*" and "*Lance-Corpl. Harbour … travelled 5,000 miles to serve his country, wounded by shrapnel 13 times*".

The 8th October saw the heading, "*Recruitment Meeting in Rushden – The Voluntary System or Conscription*". This continued with, "*A great recruiting campaign was held in Rushden, last Saturday in conformity with popular gatherings which were being held in other towns throughout the country.*" The concluding paragraph indicated that, "*If many thousands of recruits were not obtained that day, conscription was bound to come.*"

Still in self-denial, the question of what was my part in this war was ever present but as time passed I came to the realisation that choice had effectively been taken away from me – *I either volunteer or get conscripted or have shame heaped on our family by being seen as a coward*

I HAVE NO CHOICE!

The incredibly stigmatised third option and the visions of how it would affect my family were permanently in my mind. Everything I did had two versions, *what would happen to Trudy and the kids if I stayed alive by moving away and they couldn't find me and what would happen if I stayed looking after them but I'd been branded a coward?* I kept pushing it aside but there was also the persistent gut wrenching question of, *if I am killed, how will my loving Trudy and family survive?*

This wasn't helped with the news that Walter James Norman was killed on the 12th October.

On the 5th November, the *Rushed Echo* reported, "*Capt. Stocken's Stirring Appeals – Stirring appeals for recruits for the Northants Regiment were made at the Rushden theatres on Saturday night by Capt. Stocken, who in each instance, emphasized the fact that it was a Northamptonshire man's obvious duty, in joining the colours, to attach himself to his County regiment in preference to others*". My gut was permanently burning and telling me,

YOU HAVE NO CHOICE!

DECISION MADE

The pressure being applied by the Government made nearly everybody feel like an outcast and a coward if they didn't join voluntarily; I was no longer in denial, it was obvious, I have no choice, I have to go.

After the kids had gone to bed, I told Trudy of my decision to volunteer and with bear hugs, kisses and tears, she said she understood and fully supported me. She said she thought I was the bravest of men to have made the decision and it was one of the reasons why she married me. The next morning we gathered the kids and told them of my decision and although not really understanding, the very thought of me leaving them for the very first time filled them with uncertainty and endless crying.

I made my farewells to my mates at boot makers Messrs Green and Coe, in Rushden and brother George and his family came over for a leaving meal. With a very heavy heart and a gut wrenching feeling of depression, separation and uncertainty, I kissed and hugged my family tight as I left for Weymouth to join The Northamptonshire Regiment on the 19th November 1915; Christ, it was so, so hard to get on the train.

When I found out where Weymouth was, there was a bitter sweet feeling of excitement of seeing the sea for the first time and also of regret in that Trudy and the kids wouldn't be there to enjoy it with me. The feelings didn't go away when, to my utter disbelief, the train pulled in right next to the beach; the smell of, what I found out later was decomposing seaweed, was confusingly overpowering and refreshing.

Army life under training was one of utter thought confusion with me just following the crowd who were following me. Life gradually became ordered, disciplined and monotonous – parade drill, kit inspection, gymnastics, route march, football, parade drill, kit inspection, gymnastics, route march... all under the cloak of depression and loneliness and wondering if my loving Trudy's letters were telling the full truth of the utterly stable life at home. In one, Trudy said that Private Frederick Brudenell was killed on the 26th November; it wasn't easy to take my mind off the prospect that I might not return home again.

Our new uniforms or I should say, our bodies, were gradually broken in as the soft skin toughened to the constant rubbing of ill-fitting rough wool surge and hobnail boots. Scoff was monotonous in that all we seemed to eat was bully beef stew and because we were always working hard there was an ever present feeling of hunger.

We were told that they were building us into a fit and orderly fighting force where we would gain confidence, respect and comradeship and I have to admit, over time, things did fall into place, everything became second nature, respect was earned, bonds became tighter and deep comradeship established itself.

I'd never been to the seaside before and as the sense of purpose and rhythm re-entered my life, I started to re-experience the lovely early childhood feeling of being free. I didn't question Trudy's letters anymore, my stomach wasn't burning as much and I actually started feeling good about volunteering.

It wasn't long before we were on the move again to Penzance to practice trench digging on the beaches. As we moved further westward, the feelings of competence, comradeship, freedom and happiness increased. It was a lovely place to exercise the muscles that the other training hadn't found but as with all good things, this had to end and before long we were on the road to Colchester.

We were told that the next training was aimed at protecting ourselves so, in between more kit inspections and parade drill, we were given instruction in shooting, bombing, bayoneting and other niceties such as how to erect and take down barbed wire. Light-heartedly we all agreed that the Army's idea of protection was, attack and kill, attack and kill and more attack and kill.

Although we became quite proficient at bayoneting and killing dummies, the reality of having to kill somebody just didn't sink in because we were still of a mind that this was a bit of an adventure and the war couldn't last much longer.

Time slipped by with news and casualty lists filtering back from the front. Perversely, the reports were morbidly devoured to see if the threat of going to the front was diminishing and to see if any of our friends or relatives were on the lists; no name was good news.

During April, the Regiment reported:

Somme, France - Sector A.2 of trenches

April 1916

1.4 The battalion completed its tour in the trenches on the 2nd April and
2.4 returned to rest billets in BRAY, being relieved by the 7th Bn. Bedfords Regt. We exploded a mine at 4.30 a.m. on 1st April. Casualties during 1st & 2nd April, 1 killed.

BRAY SUR-SOMME

2.4
to   In billets in BRAY. Weather fine.
8.4

8.4   The Battalion marched to the trenches relieving the 7th Bedfords
to   At 2 a.m. on the 13th the enemy opened a heavy bombardment on our
14.4 centre Company. Simultaneously, two small parties attempted to raid the trenches held by our left company. They were quickly driven out, eight of them being killed. They carried off two of our men who were wounded. Captain H Podmore and 4 N.C.O.s & men were recommended for decorations and eight others for parchment letters. Casualties, 2nd Lieut. Waite, accidentally wounded, 10 killed, 34 wounded, 2 wounded and missing.

BRONFEY FARM

14.4 The battalion was relieved by the 7th Bedfords and returned to the
to   intermediate line. Hd. Qts. and 1 company at BRONFAY FARM, 3
20.4 companies in BILLON WOOD. Weather wet.

Sector A2 of trenches

20   Returned to A.2, relieving the 7th Bedfords. A fairly quiet time. Weather
to   fine. Casualties :- 2nd Lieut. A. H. P Webster, accidentally killed at
26th Brigade Bomb School and 2nd Lieut. C C. Hoare accidentally wounded at Brigade Bomb School. 1 killed, 2 wounded.

BRAY

26.4 The battalion marched back to BRAY on being relieved by the 7th
to   Bedfords
30.4 Weather, very hot

THE FRONT

Our training period and the fear of going to the front worked in opposition, decreasing and increasing respectively until finally, towards the beginning of May, orders for movement arrived.

I thought, *so this is it, my time has come. God help me and keep me safe. Nothing I can do now but keep my head down and hope that, if it does come, it will be quick. My stomach's burning again. What are Trudy and the kids doing now? I must write a letter before I sleep tonight. Don't be seen to be afraid Bob, keep busy and follow the crowd. Remember, look after your pals and they will look after you; just don't look afraid.*

As we prepared and finally mobilised, the news kept coming in:

BRAY to LA HOUSSOYE

May 1916

1.5   The 18th Division being now in Corps Reserve, the Battalion marched on May 1st to LA HOUSSOYE from BRAY-SUR-SOMME (13 miles). Weather very hot.

FRÉCHENCOURT

2.5 to 15.5   The Battalion (less "D" Coy) marched the next day 2nd May to FRÉCHENCOURT (2 miles). "D" Coy proceeded to QUERRIEUX (2 miles). All companies were employed during this period finishing the CONTAY-DAOURS Railway.

10.5   On 10th May "D" Coy marched to BRAY and were employed burying telephone cables. Captain H Podmore proceeded to England on leave and to be invested with the D.S.O awarded to him for distinguished conduct on the occasion of the German attack on the night 12th/13th April.

SAISSEVAL - BRAY - LA HOUSSOYE

15.5 to 24.5   On this date "C" Coy marched to BRAY to assist "D" Coy in their work. "A" Coy marched to CORBIE to be attached for demonstration purposes to the 18th Divl. School at LA HOUSSOYE. Lieut. Schreiner the O.C. the Coy being appointed Adjutant of the School. 2nd Lieuts. Gillott & Price joined Battn. from 3rd Bn. on 19th. Headquarters & "B" Coy marched to SAISSEVAL (18 miles). Weather wet.

The thing is, I had no idea where we were going. I knew we were heading for Le Havre but where was Le Havre and how far? I thought, *why is everything so secret? God I wish this bloody ship would stop tossing so much. My guts are burning and I feel as sick as a dog all the time. How much farther can Le Havre be?*

After what seemed like an eternity, the ship stopped rolling and we disembarked. I thought, *thank God I'm off that ship! Ha ha, it looks like we'll be taking a train. Nice to know we're not going to walk the whole way in the rain.*

24.5   Col. G. E. RIPLEY returned from England on recovering from his wounds and took over command of the Battalion from Major W T WYNDOWE.

SAISSEVAL

25.5   Draft of 38 N.C.O.s & man joined from an Entrenching Battalion.

26.5   Two drafts of 50 & 56 respectively joined from Base

From this point on, I fell into a world of introspection and self preservation - *Well, here we are, wherever this is. If it's the Front then it looks very civilised and orderly; this can't be the fighting front. I expected there to be mayhem here with people running around like headless chickens but it's quite orderly really and it doesn't look too bad.*

Ah, they're issuing us with rifles, bombs and bayonets; I wondered when they'd get round to this.

I wonder what Trudy and the kids are doing now; I wonder how they see me in their thoughts? Mmmm, right, it's time to get my head around my new surroundings, write a letter to Trudy and then try and put my family to the back of my mind.

What to write, ah, I know, My darling Trudy. I'm nearly at the Front and we've stopped off in quite a nice place. I've been told not to mention place names, sorry for this. It's a small hamlet about one third the size of Irchester and close to a few other hamlets. It's a lot like Astcote really apart from the fields being very wide and open and they give me a calm feeling of freedom.

There's a few copses and small woods around the village. The houses are stone built and single story with rusty orange wavy clay tile roofs. The main entrance door is in the middle of the front of the house and there are double windows either side; they're so familiar, cosy and welcoming. I feel this urge to go inside, sit by the hearth, smell the burnt wood and just shut the whole world out.

That said, Spring's in the air, it's a nice warm day, the trees have their shiny bottle green leaves and the crop's dark green shoots are just peeping through. Aaah, Astcote, Astcote, Astcote, how times have changed since I left you.

Please give the kids big hugs and kisses from me my love. Write to me about the village please and keep safe and happy for all our sakes, Bob.

When I think about family, I now include the Regiment and the lads. No disrespect to my darling Trudy but they're my immediate family now, the people I and they themselves rely on. We have formed a bond of comradeship that I've never known before and as I look over the swirling sea of men, I get a warm secure feeling that I'll be OK with these lads.

30.5 Major S.H. Charrington, Reserve of Officers, 15th Hussars, joined the Regiment and was appointed 2nd in Command.

1916
June
SAISSEVAL

1st The Battalion was mentioned in Gen. Sir Douglas Haig's despatch for gallant service.
4th "C" Company marched from BRAY to CORBIE and joined "D" Company there.
5th "C" and "D" Companies entrained at CORBIE for PICQUIGNY and marched to SAISSEVAL.

Special Order of the day by Bg. Gen. T. H. Soubridge C.M.G. D.S.O. Attached appendix 1

Herbert Shrives died today; I wonder how they're coping with the deaths in the village?

<u>Appendix 1</u>

SPECIAL ORDER OF THE DAY
By
Brigadier General T. H. Shoubridge, C.M.G., D.S.O., Commanding 54th. Infantry Brigade.

      The Brigade Commander wishes to congratulate sincerely the Officers, N.C.Os and men of the 7th Bn. Bedfordshire Regiment and the 6th. Bn. Northamptonshire Regiment on being mentioned as Battalions for gallant service in the Commander-in-Chief's despatch of 20th. May 1916.

      He knows that all ranks of other Units in the Brigade will join him in these congratulations and will fully appreciate the special honour these gallant battalions have gained for the 54th. Infantry Brigade.

                            H.B. STUTFIELD, Captain.
                                  Staff Captain,
                                  54th. Inf. Bde.

2nd. June 1916.

7th   The following officers joined the Battalion 2nd Lieut. Farrell R, 2nd Lieut. Jackson A.P, 2nd Lieut. Greenwood J.

PICQUIGNY

11th   The Battalion – less "A" Company left SAISSEVAL at 5-30 p.m. and marched to PICQUIGNY. "A" Company arrived at PICQUIGNY by train from CORBIE.

12th to 15th   The battalion trained in assault on trenches.

At least we're being trained in assaulting so somebody must know the whys and wherefores of this war. It's nice to be kept busy, it keeps the fear and thoughts of home away.

16th to 18th   The Brigade trained in assault on trenches : and was inspected by the Corps and Divisional Commanders.

20th   The Battalion went on a short route march.

That was interesting, a nice march in the open but undulating countryside.

21st   The Battalion performed a final assault practice over trenches.

Christ, here we go, final practice. God protect me and if it happens, make it quick. This bloody burning in my stomach is back and I'm getting worried again.

22nd   Battalion transport left for HEILLY.

23rd   Battalion marched from PICQUIGNY at 10-30 a.m. Arrived at AILLY at 11-45 a.m. Weather very hot. Train due to leave at 12-18 p.m. did not leave till 4-45 p.m. Arrived at HEILLY by train at 6-30 p.m. Marched through

and 24th   MERICOURT, "A" and "B" Corps. to BRAY where they billeted, "C" and "D" Companies and Headquarters to BRONFAY FARM into "dug-outs" – which were not reached till 2-30 a.m. Rain fell during most of afternoon and evening

At least the rain has cooled the air a bit which makes the march along the top of this ridge to Bray quite pleasant. I can see for miles and that must be the town of Albert on our left. So that is the approximate position of the Front Line but if we're marching past it, the Front Line can't be very straight. The church steeple looks a bit funny being toppled over and hanging like a broken branch.

We were mustered down by the river alongside the narrow gauge railway for a briefing by the CO. He started off by saying we were at the extreme right and southern end of the British Front Line and the next section to our right was being held by the French XX Corps.

He said we would be in the middle of our section of the attack with the 7th Division, the 11th Royal Fusiliers would be to our left and the 30th Division, the 7th Bedfords would be to our right. We would be in support of the 11th Royal Fusiliers and the 12th Middlesex would be in reserve. I found all these different Divisions, etc. a bit confusing and this was compounded with not even knowing where we were, where we were going or what we were attacking.

The CO then said that there would be a five day barrage of concentrated shelling of the enemy lines which was aimed at destroying the enemy trenches and their barbed wire. He continued with the great news that after this, there would be nothing left of the Bosche and our "attack" would be like a Sunday walk in the park.

Although orders were too slowly walk in formation across no-man's-land and occupy what was left of the enemy trenches, we, just in case things didn't go so well, were going to do it a bit different and move in small blobs at irregular intervals and at our own speeds.

Well, I thought, *that sounds good, perhaps this war isn't going to be as tough as I'd thought; a Sunday walk in the park, mmmm, sounds just about right to me.*

The CO went on to say that because it was considered an occupying exercise, we would be carrying a bit of excess gear which we would need in order to consolidate the area. As a Sergeant demonstrated the moves, he said that because there wouldn't be any need to use our rifles we were to carry them a few inches in front of and across our chest with our bayonets fixed and pointing towards the sky.

Those in command seemed very happy with the plan and this cheered us up but the CO warned us to be ready at 2 a.m. for the biggest barrage that had ever been fired in history. *Mmmm, I thought, this should be good.*

BRONFAY FARM

24th   Artillery bombardment of enemy trenches commenced about 2 a.m.

Well, we were ready, or so we thought. There was an instinctive duck of protection and within seconds I could hardly hear myself think. I thought, *I pity the poor bastards under that lot but at least it'll make our life easier; give it to em lads – poor buggers.*

25th   Reconnaissance by Officers of "forming-up" trenches of battalion for coming attack.

The bombardment's still going – poor buggers. Bloody lice; the itching's getting through to me and the hot weather isn't helping either.

I thought the scoff wouldn't be as good but I can't complain really because at least it's hot. I suppose the best stuff's being taken as it passes down the line to us poor buggers in the trenches. Same old bully beef, biscuits and brew with a slight taste of petrol. I suppose the rum ration every morning could be considered a treat, that is, if you like rum with tea that has a slight hint of petrol. I wonder if I'll ever get used to it?

I thought they were pulling my leg when they described the size of the rats until I saw one of the buggers – huge it was, nearly the size of a small cat; brrrrrrr, can't stand the bloody things.

26th   Work on "forming-up" trenches.

It's still going – surely nothing's going to survive this bombardment. I see a 240mm heavy trench mortar has arrived – more punishment for the Bosche.

27th   All Officers valises and heavy kits were sent back to 1st line transport.

The main barrage is continuing and being added too by the trench mortars. That's another seven shells from that mortar – I can't help but feel for them poor buggers over there.

28th   Rained hard all day and condition of trenches became very bad –
Forming up trenches completed, wire on our line of advance removed and all preparations for the attack completed

This is it, THE - BIG – PUSH, that is if we can walk in this bloody thick sticky mud.

I can't imagine anybody being left alive over there after the pounding we gave them. Love you my Trudy, thinking of you and the kids playing in Irchester. God protect me and the lads.

When I think back now, this is where I first experienced the feeling of protective isolation engulfing me in a muffled bubble of spatial awareness; my bubble touching their bubbles within the greater bubble. I believe this was the point that my mind finally locked into my training and it was able to instantly and unconsciously adapt to any situation it found itself in.

In slow motion, I experienced my mind focusing and shrinking my need for protection to the outer layer of my skin and taking on a totally disciplined control of my activities. I just knew what I had to do and I did it in this bubble that muffled everything apart from succinct orders that I instinctively knew were meant for me; a truly astonishing world to be in.

– It was thought that the attack would start tomorrow, but, probably owing to the weather – instructions were received that zero hour would be postponed for 48 hours.

After all that work, the attack's been called off. I'm not happy. My mind's beginning to release the tension and switch it's focus on my burning stomach. My ears are ringing, I'm calf high in mud in the rain and I'm not happy, at all. We get all worked up for the attack and then we're expected to try and release the tension and calm down; I wish we could get on with it because the waiting's a killer in itself.

We've been told that the barrage will continue. The trench mortar lads have got the range to a tee now and they've just sent over another 10 shells to add to the Bosche's misery. Surely there's nothing else to kill over there. The noise has certainly affected my hearing and my head's ringing like St Katharine's bells on Sunday morning.

29th   Weather cleared and ground began to dry up.

The downpour changes from water to metal as the rain eases and the mortars open up again. Forty, forty one, forty two...forty two more mortars from the local team and I have to admit, after all this, it can only be a simple walk in the park.

30th   See July 1st.

Another 34 mortars delivered. I wonder what hell looks like over there? Well, tomorrow we'll see...

G Ripley   Colonel
ommdg. 6th (S) Bn. Northamptonshire Regiment

BATTLE OF THE SOMME 1 JULY – 18 NOVEMBER 1916

For actual sketches, please refer to pages 75 & 76 of the 6th (S) Northamptonshire Regiment War Diary
WO-95-2044-2_1

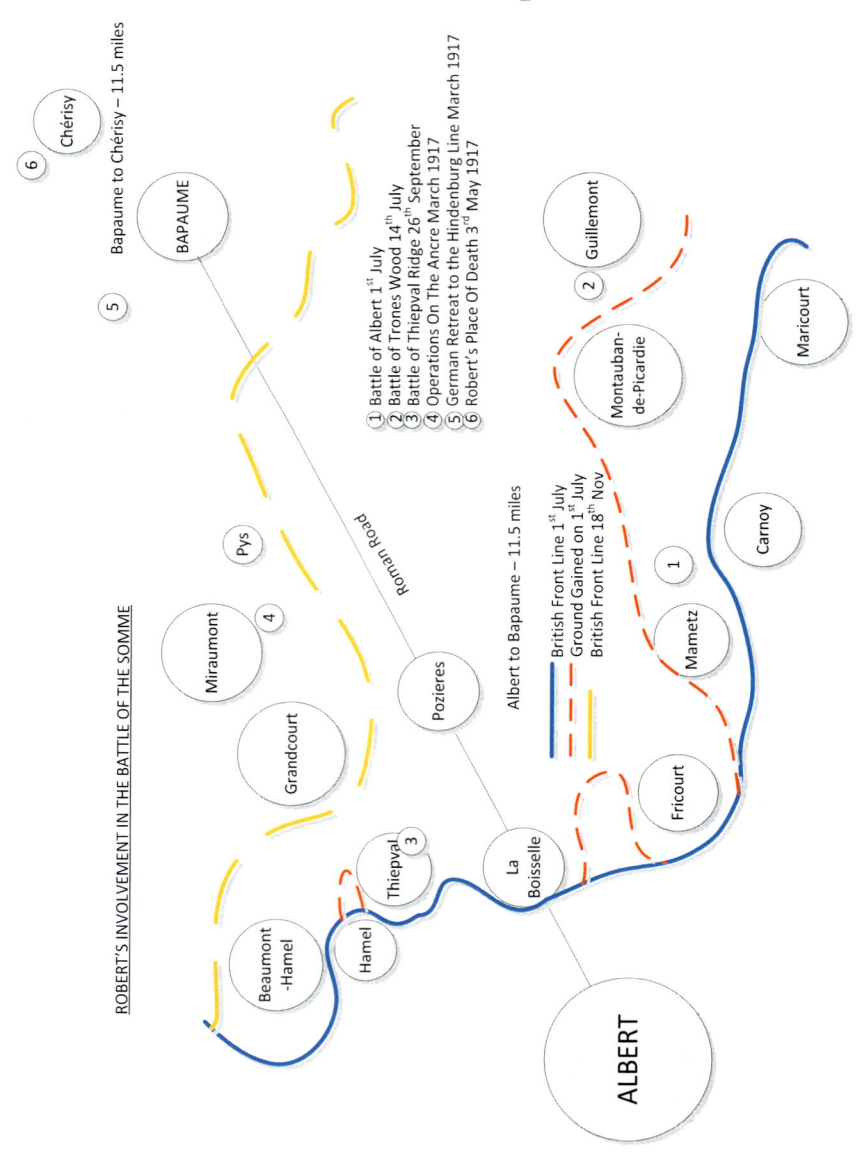

① Battle of Albert 1st July
② Battle of Trones Wood 14th July
③ Battle of Thiepval Ridge 26th September
④ Operations On The Ancre March 1917
⑤ German Retreat to the Hindenburg Line March 1917
⑥ Robert's Place Of Death 3rd May 1917

ROBERT'S INVOLVEMENT IN THE BATTLE OF THE SOMME

Bapaume to Chérisy – 11.5 miles
Albert to Bapaume – 11.5 miles

British Front Line 1st July
Ground Gained on 1st July
British Front Line 18th Nov

Roman Road

Chérisy, BAPAUME, Guillemont, Maricourt, Montauban-de-Picardie, Miraumont, Pys, Carnoy, Grandcourt, Pozieres, Mametz, Thiepval, La Boisselle, Fricourt, Beaumont-Hamel, Hamel, ALBERT

THE BATTLE OF ALBERT

1916   Operation Orders for the attack and sketch map attached.

Appendix D

18th Division, 54th Infantry Brigade,
6th (S) Bn, The Northamptonshire Regiment
GENERAL MAP OF ATTACK 1ST JULY 1916
SPECIAL MAP ISSUED TO COMPANY COMMANDERS

Reproduced to show 6th Northants involvement.

MONTAUBAN DE- PICARDIE

Div. Line 18th & 30th Divisions

CARNOY

Pommiers Trench

FINAL OBJECTIVE of 54th & 6th Northants

Pommiers Redoubt

Pommiers Lane

Red line

Strong points I- VII

Maple Trench

Blue line

VII

VI

vine 54th Right & Left

V

IV

III

Black Alley

Div. Line 54th & 53rd I.B.

54th IB
6th Northants

Bucket Trench

Div. Line 91st & 54th I.B.

MAMETZ

31

SECRET OPERATIONAL ORDER~~X~~ No. 10   No 1

by Colonel G.E. Ripley,
Commanding 6th (S) Bn. Northamptonshire Regiment   22. 6. 16

Appendix 2

Reference Special Map issued to Company Commanders

1. **GENERAL PLAN.**

    A decisive battle which the 18th Division will take a prominent part will be fought shortly. The 30th Division (13th Corps) will attack on the right and the 7th Division (15th Corps) on the left of the 18th Division.

    Other Corps will attack EASTWARD on the left.

    Dividing lines between Units are marked on map thus:-

    ....   The final objective of the 18th Division is marked
    "Final Objective".   The 55th Brigade will be on the right, 53rd Centre and the 54th left of the 18th Division all abreast. The 91st Brigade (7th Division) will be on immediate left of the 54th Bde. The attack will be preceded by a five days bombardment by all calibre of guns and mortars. The days will be designated by letters of the alphabet and the assault will be carried out on "Z" day. The attack will be divided into three phases as shown on map.

    1st Phase········ Red Line.
    2nd Phase········ ~~Green Line~~. Red & Blue
    3rd Phase········ Blue Line.

    The ~~Green~~ Line [red & blue] and that portion of the red line included in the frontages of the 18th and 30th Divisions from junction of POMMIERS LANE and POMMIERS TRENCH EASTWARDS must be held at all costs for a prolonged period against counter-attack.

2. TASK OF 54th INFANTRY BRIGADE.

The objective of the 54th Infantry Brigade will be:-

First Objective.   Junction of POMMIERS TRENCH with POPOFF LANE – POMMIERS TRENCH to junction with **BLACK ALLEY** – BUCKET TRENCH to a point 120 yards west of XXXXX XXXXX BLACK ALLEY.

Second Objective.   Point (A.1.B.8.1) POMMIERS LANE – JUNCTION OF POMMIERS LANE and MAPLE TRENCH – POMMIERS REDOUBT-MAPLE TRENCH to its junction with BEETLE ALLEY.

Third Objective.

A line from point S.26.A.8.3 through point S.26.A.2.2. to the right of 91st Brigade about point S.25.b.3.0.

In capturing these objectives the following are of Vital importance   :-

   (a) To secure BLACK ALLEY as a defensive flank to the 18th DIV. and should occasion arise <u>to hold it at all costs.</u>
   (b) To consolidate and hold the second objective at all costs even if MONTAUBAN and MAMETZ should not be captured.
   (c) To consolidate that portion of BEETLE ALLEY from S.25.d.98.27 to junction of MAPLE TRENCH.

3. TASK OF 6th BN. NORTHAMPTONSHIRE REGIMENT.

The 6th (S) Bn. Northamptonshire Regiment will act as third or supporting Battalion to the Brigade.

Their role is to support the assaulting Battalions if required as far as the line MAPLE TRENCH-POMMIERS REDOUBT. When this line is made good the duty of the Battalion is to put in a state of defence a line Point II (junction of BUND TRENCH and BLACK ALLEY) to junction of BLACK ALLEY and MAPLE TRENCH on the West and on the North from Point 5 (junction of MAPLE TRENCH and BEETLE ALLEY) EASTWARDS to POMMIERS REDOUBT inclusive and from the latter to the Strong Point in POMMIERS ~~TRENCH~~ LANE established by the 53rd Brigade.

4. **FLANKS.**

    The flanks of the Brigade are shown in map.

5. **DISPOSITIONS.**

    During the waiting period the Battalion will be at BRONFAY FARM. Prior to the attack the Battalion will occupy the Trenches in CARNOY. Bn. Headquarters will be at PICCADILLY.

6. **THE ATTACK.** At

    ~~The~~ ZERO on "Z" day, "A" and "B" Coys will move forward and occupy GLASGOW ROAD and ~~HIGH~~ HYDE ROAD **xxx** EAST and WEST.

    They will move in small "blobs" at irregular intervals and distances.

    "A" Coy will be on the right and "B" Coy on the left, the two Companies covering the whole front. "D" Coy will follow in rear of "A" and "B" in the same irregular formation and will cover the whole Brigade front.

    "A" and "B" Coys will push forward behind the assaulting Battalions and will enter EMDEN and ASUSTRIAN TRENCHES when the assaulting Battalions have vacated them. They will then follow the assaulting Battalions and take over the line MAPLE TRENCH – POMMIERS REDOUBT when the assaulting Battalions have made good BEETLE ALLEY with two Companies and pushed forward their other two Coys to the final objective. Every Commander from Platoon upwards will retain a reserve on his hands for the unexpected.

7. **STRONG POINTS.**

    "A" Coy will take over POMMIERS REDOUBT (S.P. VII) with three platoons and Coy Headquarters. The remaining platoon will hold S.P. VI in POMMIERS TRENCH.

    "B" Coy will take over the JUNCTION BEETLE ALLEY – MAPLE

TRENCH (S.P.V) JUNGLE BLACK ALLEY – BUCKET TRENCH (S.P. IV) JUNCTION BLACK ALLEY – POMMIERS TRENCH (S.P. III). The remaining platoon will hold MAPLE TRENCH between S.P.V. and VII. Coy Headquarters will be at S.P. IV.

"D" Coy will send 1 platoon to hold POMMIERS TRENCH from VI to its JUNCTION with POPOFF LANE whilst two platoons to hold POMMIERS TRENCH from VI to its JUNCTION with BLACK ALLEY. The fourth Platoon will take over the CIRCUS (S.P.II). Coy Headquarters will be at ~~VI.~~2 Battalion Headquarters will be at TRIANGLE.

These strong points will be prepared for allround defence and strengthened with wire. They will be held at any cost. Coys will send Officers or N.C.OS to take over their STRONG POINTS before the assaulting Battalions vacate them.

STRONG POINTS to be constructed by Brigade on our right and left are shown thus – ①

8. DU<u>GOUT CLEARING PARTIES</u>. two

"C" Coy will detail ~~one~~ platoons to report to O.C.7th Beds and 2 platoon to report to O.C 11th Royal Fusiliers. They will be used as dugout clearing parties. They will be equipped as shown in appendix B.

9. C<u>ARRYING PARTIES</u>.

"C" Coy will detail one platoon to go to "A" Dump and report to officer in charge and one platoon to report to Officer in charge "B" Dump xxx for carrying.

All these parties will be in position by ZERO.

10. <u>ROYAL ENGINEERS</u>.

1 Section Royal Engineers will assist in construction of S.P. II, III, IV, and V.

One section R.E. will assist in consolidation of 2nd objective and in construction of S.P. V and VII.

11. MACHINE GUNS.

Four Vickers guns will go with the assaulting Battalions. Eight guns will advance in rear and under cover of the 6th Northants Regt. Two of these will go to POMMIERS REDOUBT, two to S.P. V, two to S.P. VI and one each to S.P. II and III.

There will be no Vickers gun in S.P. IV.

12. STOKES GUNS.

Twelve guns will be in position in our front line. When S.P. II, III, IV, V, VI and VII xxx are consolidated one gun will move forward to each. The Hd. Qrs of 54th T.M.B. will be with Hd. Qrs 6th Northants Regt.

13. BOSCHE   COUNTER ATTACK.

The BOSCHE delivers small Counter attacks with platoons or Companies immediately hostile troops gain their objectives. These small counter attacks have had far reaching results and must be specially guarded against. To meet these small counter attacks the Reserves in the hands of Platoon and Coy Commanders will be of the greatest value.

14. RELIEFS.

All Troops must clearly understand that nor reliefs can be expected until their final objectives have been efficiently consolidated.

15. DUMPS.

The supply of all ammunition, Grenades, R.E. material etc., will be worked from a series of Dumps. These are marked on map. Those at "A" and "B" will be considered advanced Dumps, that at "C" advanced Brigade Reserve Dump and that at "D" Brigade Dump. The advanced dumps will move forward by stages. Brigade will keep these Dumps full and Battalion will draw stores for these dumps.

Contents are shown in appendix "C".

"A" and "B" Dump will open at TRIANGLE and CIRCUS respectively as early as possible after first objective is gained. They will move forward to POMMIERS REDOUBT and S.P. IV after the x capture of second objective.

Rations and water will not be carried forward till nightfall.

16. TOOLS.

50% of "A", "B" and "D" Coys will carry tools in the proportion of two shovels to one pick. Tools will be carried in a vertical position on mans' back. A reserve of tools will be kept at "C" Dump from which Companies may draw to meet their requirements.

17. AMMUNITION CARRIERS.

Each Lewis Gun team will be strengthened by four Lewis Reserve gunners to carry S.A.A.

18. WATER.

The supply of water during and after the assault will be difficult. All water bottles must be full at ZERO hour and all ranks must practice the greatest restraint in drinking water. The normal supply will be from the Well, CARNOY and pipes in CARNOY. Reserve Storage tanks have been placed in the Russian Saps at "A" and "B" Dumps. 250 petrol tins have also been placed at each of these Dumps.

19. MEDICAL ARRANGEMENTS.

The 55th Field Ambulance will collect all wounded in the Division. Advanced dressing stations will be established at the following points :-

(A) In dugouts at West end of BRICK ALLEY, CARNOY for wounded of 53rd and 54th Brigades. (accommodation for 200 S.C.)

(B) In dugouts at BRONFAY FARM for local and walking cases,

accommodation 50.

All walking cases will be directed to the Advanced Dressing Station at CARNOY and from there will proceed via CARNOY AVENUE to BRONFAY FARM Dressing station. Regimental aid posts will be established as shown in map. Wounded will be conveyed from these posts to the nearest advanced dressing station by Regimental stretcher bearers.

Wounded cases in enemy trenches will be collected into suitable dugouts by Regimental Medical Officers. These dugouts must be marked and their positions notified to 55th Field Amb.

In addition to Eight stretchers per Battalion 16 R.A.M.C. stretchers will be stored near each Regimental Aid Post and used by both R.A.M.C. and Regimental bearers for bringNing in cases.

20 XXXX <u>VETERINARY</u>.

The Veterinary Officer in charge of 83rd Brigade R.F.A. is responsible for the TRth Brigade.

54

21. <u>PRISONERS</u>.

Prisoners will be sent back in batches to the Brigade Dump and thence to the Advanced Divl. collecting station at BILLON FARM. They will be marched <u>across the open</u> and not down communication trenches. Escorts to BILLON Farm will be found by the Battalions which take the prisoners the men rejoining their Units under proper control as soon as possible. The prisoners will be taken in batches of 100 with 10% escort. Slightly wounded men can be used for escort. Prisoners must be disarmed and searched for concealed weapons and documents immediately after capture before being marched off and <u>Officers must be separated from the rank and file immediately</u>.

Prisoners will be searched for documents and examined under Divl. arrangements at Divl. Collecting Station. <u>Immediate information must be sent bach concerning the identification of Regiments opposed to us</u>.

22. **CAPTURED GUNS.**

When hostile guns are captured the following procedure will be adopted.

(a) Report to Bn. Headquarters number and nature of guns captured.

(b) Detail parties to manhandle them to the nearest position where gun teams can be hooked.

(c) Report exact position where teams are required and number of teams necessary.

23. **OFFICERS.**

The following Officers will accompany the Battalion:-

Colonel G.E. Ripley......................In command.
Captain D.L. Evans.......................Adjutant.
Major G.M. Clark.........................O.C. "C" Coy.
Capt. H Podmore.........................O.C. "D" Coy.
Capt. F.S. Neville..........................O.C. "B" Coy.
Capt. O.D. Schreiner....................O.C. "A" Coy.
Lieut. G.G.H. Batty......................."B" Coy.
" G. Shankster...................... Lewis Gun Officer.
" H.M. Eldridge..................... Bombing Officer.
" J.D. Unwin.......................... "D" Coy.
2nd Lt. N.C. Hamilton.................. "B" Coy.
" G.L. Woulfe....................... "A" "
" L.G. Crook......................... "C" "
" F.G.B. Lys........................... "C" "
" D.M. Heriz-Smith............... "A" "
" C.G. Keys........................... "A" "
" J. Greenwood.................... "B" "
" A.V. Jackson....................... "C" "
" B.C. Gillott......................... O.C. Signals
" R.T. Price........................... "D" Coy.

Major S.H. Charrington will be employed as Liason Officer at Bde.H.Qrs and will be accomodated in a dugout at BRONFAY FARM. The Left group R.A. will arrange for his Messing.

~~The following Officers will be with 1st Line Transport :-~~

The following will be with the 1st Line Transport.

    Capt. Shepherd S.F.
    Lieut Arnold   J.F.
    2nd Lt. Margoliouth   H.M.
    "   "   Redhead   H.A.
    "   "   Higham   P.H.
    "   "   Hayward   H.W.
    "   "   Farrell   R.
    Lieut Fowler   W.H.
    "   Beasley   J.N.

The following will be at Schools :-

    Lieut Wilcox   F.A.C.   Divl.
    2nd Lt. Walker   F.D.S   "
    "   "   Chatham   G.K.   "
    "   "   Fawkes   R.B.   Army

24. COLLECTION OF INTELLIGENCE.

Two men will be attached to each assaulting Battalion to collect documents etc., in enemy trenches. They will each carry a sack with a red white and blue bullseye on each side of it.

25. STRAGGLERS.

Regimental Police will control traffic in trenches and will check stragglers moving to the rear. They will take numbers, names and Units of all stragglers and march them back in parties to their Units. Their duties will be detailed by Brigade.

26. RATIONS.
Normal system of supply will continue throughout operations.

Rations will be delivered to the 1st Line Transport, GROVE-TOWN, who will convey same to BRONFAY FARM where they will be transferred to Tramline.

Reserve rations are dumped in "A" and "B" Dumps and in CARNOY to meet any unforeseen contingency. These will only be issued under Bde Orders.

27. COMMUNICATION TRENCHES.
The Main UP trench will be **XXXXX** PIONEER AVENUE commencing at BRONFAY FARM.

The Main DOWN Trench (evacuation) trench will be MAIDSTONE-CARNOY AVENUE.

28. ARTILLERY FLAGS.
Every Platoon will carry two red and yellow Artillery flags. These will be waved to and fro for a short period by the leading line to show our Artillery how far the attack has progressed. On no account will any flag be stuck in the ground.

These flags will not be waved at any position in advance of POMMIERS REDOUBT.

29. EQUIPMENT. TO BE CARRIED ON THE MAN.
Every man will carry :-
Rifle and equipment(less pack) one bandolier in addition to his equipment ammunition, 170 rounds. in all
One day's ration and one iron ration.
One waterproof sheet, two sandbags, one white enamel disc hung on the back or yellow patch. Two smoke helmets.
NOTE.   The haversack will be carried on back.
Grenadiers will carry 50 rounds S.A.A. only.

30. CASUALTIES.

Casualties will be reported to Bn.Hd.Qrs as soon as possible. They should be reported under the heading of Officers, Other ranks. Numbers only are required for these frequent estimates, but at 2 p.m. each day the correct names of casualties should be sent in correct as far as possible. The day will be reckoned from 12 noon to 12 noon. Attention is called to S.C. 113 issued to Coy~~x~~ Commanders.

31. COMMUNICATIONS.

(a). Telephonic. Brigade Telephone Stations will be established at Hd.Qrs of the two assaulting Battalions and the 3rd Battalion in our own Trenches. These will be Signal Offices worked by Bde operators. There will be a permanent exchange at CARNOY. Communication with Artillery can be obtained through CARNOY EXCHANGE or through ~~Battalion~~ Brigade Hd.Qrs. The 6th Northants Regt. will take over the Signal Office at the TRIANGLE from the 7th Beds Regt. when the Hd.Qrs move there. When the second objective is captured the Bde Signals will open at Bde Signal Station at TRIANGLE they will move forward to POMMIERS REDOUBT when circumstances admit. If telephonic communication breaks down between station messages will be sent back by runner to the nearest exchange that is in communication with Bde.Hd.Qrs and telephone from there.

(b) VISUAL. A Divl. Reading station will be established at A.19.b.3.9 from this the German lines up to POMMIERS TRENCH are under observation and Signallers will be on the lookout day and night. The ground beyongd POMMIERS TRENCH is not visible from this station.

Signallers with Coy and Bn.Hd.Qrs will carry discs and a few flags will be taken forward by Battn.Hd.Qrs. All messages will be sent "DD" and repeated twice. They should therefore be as sgort as possible. The 6th Northants will establish a Visual Station at the TRIANGLE as soon as they reach there and will provide a visual station at VI S.P. POMMIERS TRENCH as soon as the second objective is captured. Messages coming back by runner ~~and~~ from assaulting battalions may be sent from the last named station by visual.

As many Signallers as possible to carry electric torches by night.

(c) <u>Contact Aeroplane Patrols</u>.

Every man will carry one red flare. One special Signalling ~~man~~ lamp 1 panel and one ground sheet will be carried by Bn.Hd.Qr. Signallers.

The ground sheet will be put out as soonas Hd.Qrs reach *a* new position but should only be unfolded when one of our own aeroplanes is over the line.

XIIIth and XVth Corps aeroplanes will be of type B.E.2.C. will have a broad black band and on each lower plane. The method of communication with aeroplanes will be that already practiced.

(d) <u>RUnners</u>.

Bde will send Runners to CIRC~~U~~LE and TRIANGLE and a Bde Runner Post will be established at TRIANGLE when second objective is captured.

Permanent Brigade Runner Posts will be established at Signal Office, CARNOY at PICADILLY and at Bde.Hd.Qrs. All important messages must be sent by Runners in pairs.

(e) <u>General</u>. The Bn. Signal Officer will ascertain all details from Bde Signal Officer.

All Signaller and runners will be under the Battn.Signal Officer.

Officers should always speak on telephone themselves if possible or else **xxxxx** write down messages and sign them. Signallers are ordered not to accept messages unless signed by an Officer, or N.C.O. or man commanding a Unit. All messages must **xx** have time and place on them and should be as short as possible. Constant communication must be kept up with the assaulting Bns.and the Bns. on the right and left of the Bde. All informationx should be sent back to Bn.Hd.Qrs. immediately

32. MISCELLANEOUS.

No maps showing our own trenches or important papers will be carried by Officers and men taking part in the attack.

Headquarters.

The Hd.Qrs 6th Northants Regt will open at TRIANGLE when that Bn. takes over the second objective and S.P I to VII from assaulting Battalions.

Wire.

All our wire in front and behind our Front line will be cleared by 7th Beds and 11th Royal Fusiliers.

(Sgd)   D.L. Evans, Capt & Actg Adjt.
6th (S) Bn. Northamptonshire Regiment.

Copies Issued to :-

1. C.O.
2. Brigade.
3. O.C. "A" Coy.
4. O.C. "B"   "
5. O.C. "C"   "
6. O.C. "D"   "
7. Signals Officer

APPENDIX "A"   Position of Units 54th Inf.Bde
immediately before ZERO hour.

UNIT	POSITION	FRONTAGE	BATTN.H.Q	REMARKS
11th R.F. (also 2 Vickers Guns & 2 Stokes Mortars)	Forming up trenches Left assaulting Battn.	Chester St. (exclusive) F.12.C.20.90 to Trench Junction (inclusive) F.12.C.8590	LONDON ROAD & BROWN STREET JUNCTION.	Each Assaulting Bn. is on 2 Coy front. 1st Trnch X 4 pltns. 2nd " - 4 " 3rd " - 1 Coy (& 1 pltn N'hants as dug-out Clearing party 4th Trnch - 1 Coy.
7th Beds XXXXXX as 11th R.F.	ditto	Trench Junction (exclusive) F.12.C.85.90 to YORK Road (exclusive) A.7.d.54.82.	NEW CUT.	ditto
6th N'hants (less 4 platoons).	In old Trenches. Just W of CARNOY	------------------	PICCADILLY	As in attached Orders.
12th Bn. Midd'x R.	In dug-outs in CARNOY	------------------	A.2 Hd.Qrs, CARNOY	Reserve Battalion

(1)

Unit.	POSITION	HEADQUARTERS	REMARKS
54th M.G.C.	2 guns in Tunnelled saps 2 guns with 11th R.F. 2 guns with 7th Beds. 4 guns with 6th N'hants. 6 guns in CAFTET WOOD	A.2 Hd.Qrs. CARNOY	
54th T.M.B. & 1 sectn 26th T.M.B.	2 mortars with 11th R.F. 2 mortars with 7th Beds. 8~2~ mortars in position for bombardment	Ditto	
2 sectns R.E.	CARNOY.		
2 Pltns Suss Pioneers	CARNOY		
54th Bde. H.Q.	At Bde Battle Hd.Qrs at F.24.C.55 near BILLON FARM		

APPENDIX "B"   GRENADES.

XXX ALL BATTALIONS.	HOW CARRIED.	WHERE STORED BEFORE THE ATTACK.	WHEN TO BE DRAWN.	REMARKS.
Each Pltn Bombg section of 8 men.	10 gdes on each man.	Carried on the man.	Now in possession of Battns.	
Rifle Gdes. 10 per Pltn. Bombg section	On N.C.O. i/c Pltn. Bombg Section.	At Coy Hd.Qrs in Forming up trenches.	When forming up.	3rd & 4th Bns. will draw 160 rifle gdes each from A.2 Sub-section H.Q. CARNOY before moving fwd.
THE TWO ASSAULTING BNS ONLY Same per Plat-oon bombg Sec. each carrying a bucket containing 15 MILLS Gdes.	In Bucket	At Coy H.Qrs. in forming up trenches	When formg up.	Two assaulting Battalions only.
50% strength of the 2 pltns of 3rd Bn. employed as dug-out clearg parties (say 20 men per pltn) each carryg a bucket containing 18 MILLS Gdes.	in Bucket.	"C" Dump	From "C" Dump when forming up.	Two Platoons.

"B" Dumped at the hour of assault	"A" DUMP .... 2.490 MILLS Grenades
	                                                            390 Rifle "
	"B" DUMP .... 2,490 MILLS Grenades
	                                                            390 Rifle "
	"C" (Advanced Bde) DUMP .... 4, 280 MILLS Grenades
	                                                            2 240 Rifle "
	"D" (Bde Reserve) DUMP .... N I L
	
	Mobile Reserve on limbered wagon with 1st Line Transport at 768 MILLS Grenades per Battalion .... 3,072 MILLS.
	                                        Total ....
	                                            13,352			

APPENDIX "C"   DUMPS.

OFFICER IN CHARGE.	CONTENTS	REMARKS.
	"A"	
Lieut Tilton, 7th Bedfors Regt.	950 MILLS GRENADES 1540 MILLS " 390 Rifle " 100 Boxes S.A.A. 40 Boxes S.A.A. (Reserve For LEWIS GUNS). 250 Petrol tins of water Water tanks. 560 rounds STOKES ammn. 2000 Rations. Material for rapid wiring.	(At present at A.2 Grenade Store).
	"B"	
Lieut Rendle. 11th R.Rus.	Same as "A" Dump.	
	"C"	
Lieut Covell 7th Bedford Regt.	4280 Mills Grenades. 240 Rifle " 4000 Rations. Picks. Shovals. R.E.Material. 80 Boxes S.A.A. (Reserve For LEWIS GUNS).	
	"D" (Brigade Dump).	
Lieut Whiteman. 11th R. Fus.	170 Boxes S.A.A. (Div.Res) 62 " S.A.A. (Div.Res) For M.G.Coy. 8000 Rations. 1000 Reserve Smoke Helmets.	

47

7. <u>PLAN OF ATTACK</u>   Amendment from O.O. 18 of 27·6·16

(C) The remaining two platoons of the 3rd Coy 6th Northants Regt will carry forward small manloads of R.E Stores. These will be deposited at the TRIANGLE. As soon as platoons reach that point they will rejoin their battalion. The latter platoons must not be confused with those permanently allotted to A and B units.

COPY

SECRET   EXTRACT FROM   O.O. 18   of 27·6·16

1. <u>INFORMATION.</u>

    (a) <u>Enemy</u>.

        The XII Div. VI German Corps is holding the line from the RIVER SOMME to FRICOURT.

        The 62nd Inf. Regt. holds from the MARICOURT – HARDECOURT to the CARNOY – MONTAUBAN ROAD.

        The 23rd Inf. Regt. holds from the latter Road to FRICOURT.

    (b) <u>Our own Troops.</u>

        Following further information regarding the objective of the Fourth Army as a whole are published.

        After the capture and consolidation of the objective laid down for the first days operations preparations have been made for a further advance to the line MONTAUBAN – BAZENTIN le GRAND – MARTINPUICH. This advance will be affected by the 15th and 3rd Corps passing across the front of the 18th Division.

        In order that this operation may be successfully carried out, it will be necessary for the 18th Division to hold the line to its furthermost objective for at least three days without being relieved.

        The positions of neighbouring Corps and Divisions on the flanks of the 18th Division remain as described in Operation Order No 17.

        The 9th Division is in XIII Corps Reserve

What a lovely summer's morning, apart from the shelling that is. Another 12 shells from of our local mortars adding to the Bosche's misery. The thought of the destruction over the past few days and the warm sun on my back has calmed my nerves. The news is that the trench mortar guys have severely damaged the German trenches and the barbed wire has just about been destroyed, so it looks like they were right, it will be a walk in the park.

I'm getting a sort of bubble feeling again as our attack orders are read to us. I hope somebody knows what'll actually happen because it seems bloody complicated to me. The bit I did understand was that me and the lads are to go through the middle between Mametz and Montauban and we're to hold the positions for 3 days. Well, if there's going to be nobody alive over there that should be pretty easy. I can't understand why they told us to write our wills if it's going to be that easy – a bit over cautious I think.

At least the waiting's over and after the shelling we've given them, there shouldn't be anybody left alive to shoot back. Perhaps this war won't be as bad as everybody makes out; perhaps the tide has turned.

Cor,   silence,   apart from the ringing in my head.

This consolidation gear's heavier than they said it would be. Fix bayonets ordered. I instantly ducked for protection as I thought, *what-the-hell-was-that?! That's a hell of an explosion.* As my mind recovered, the ground moved under my feet and I though, *the shudders are going right up my legs and my helmet's rattling my brain. The mining guys' efforts seem to have paid off. Nearly 07:30, I'm tense and I feel like I'm ready to go.*

Another! That one sounded and felt bigger than the one 10 minutes ago. Surely, there can't be anybody left over there.

Whistles blowing, here we go, love you my Trudy...

July 1st Narrative of the part taken by the 6th (Service) Battalion, Northamptonshire Rgt. in the attack on the German position between MAMETZ and MONTAUBAN :-

The 54th Brigade were the left brigade of the 18th division, which attacked the German position between MAMETZ (exclusive) and MONTAUBAN (inclusive) with three brigades in the front line. The first objective of the 54th Brigade was from the POMMIERS REDOUBT (inclusive) on the right to the junction of BEETLE ALLEY and MAPLE TRENCH (inclusive) on the left. The final objective was the ridge overlooking CATERPILLAR WOOD and WILLOW BROOK, demarcated by the ~~gree~~ blue line on the attached map. The 91st Brigade, 7th Division were on our left and the 53rd Brigade, 18th Division on our right. The 11th Royal Fusiliers on the left and the 7th Bedfordshires Rgt. on the right formed the front line of the 54th Brigade.

The 6th Battalion Northamptonshire Rgt. ~~wer~~ (less six platoons) were the 3rd or supporting battalion and also formed one company as "dug-out" clearing parties which were attached to the Royal Fusiliers and Bedfords and cleared the "dug-outs" in the ~~th~~ German trenches. The three remaining platoons acted as carrying parties to the brigade.

The 12th Middlesex Rgt. were the Brigade Reserve.

The Brigade had undergone a week's previous training over ground laid out on the plan of the German trenches to be attacked and were in fine fettle when the day arrived.

The German trenches and wire entanglement had been battered for seven days by our intense artillery bombardment.

On the night preceding the launching of the attack (June 30th – July 1st) the two battalions in the front line were accommodated in our four front line trenches.

The 6th Northamptonshire Rgt. (less six platoons) moved from BRONFAY FARM about 11-30 p.m. on 30th June and occupied their forming-up trenches as follows – A Coy. right Coy. supporting the Bedfordshire Rgt. in trenches N & N.W. of CARNOY.

B. Coy. left Coy supporting the Royal Fusiliers in trenches in CAFTET WOOD – D Coy. (less 2 platoons) with a portion of Battalion Hqrs. were in reserve and were concealed in trenches in the same wood.

It was no easy matter for these companies in such a restricted area to debouch from the wood and get into position for the advance as there were many trenches to cross and gaps in our wire entanglements to be negotiated. The terrain however had been carefully reconnoitred by officers and section commanders on previous nights and trenches had been bridged and wire cut.

At half-an-hour after zero hour (8 a.m.) the regiment in lines of half platoons at about 60 paces interval and 150 paces distance found themselves launched to the attack. They had to change direction slightly to the right and open out, soon after moving off, but this was successfully accomplished. The ~~reg~~ battalion advanced as steadily as if they were on the parade ground, their instructions being that it was not to halt until the enemy second trench AUSTRIAN SUPPORT was reached.

All companies came under a heavy artillery barrage before our rear trench HYDE ROAD WEST was reached, but they continued to move forward with admiral coolness, A Coy. even checking in "no man's land" to correct their direction. The two leading companies arrived simultaneously at the EMDEN and AUSTRIAN support trenches.

A halt of 40 minutes here took place, during which the left Coy. and bombing parties were detached and sent up BLACK ALLEY. At the same time (8-20 a.m.) the right platoon of A Coy. had reached BUND TRENCH and were followed 20 minutes later by the 2nd platoon who moved to avoid artillery fire.

From BUND TRENCH to POMMIER TRENCH both companies came under a heavy artillery fire and suffered considerably and here Captain Neville commanding B Coy. was wounded. A Coy. on reaching POMMIER TRENCH immediately began making strong point (VI). The three remaining platoons proceeding to POMMIERS REDOUBT and consolidated that on evacuation by the Bedfords – B Coy. moved up at the same time and started to consolidate their allotted strong points as follows :-

    1 platoon to No. III Strong Point
    1   " " MAPLE TRENCH
    1   " " No. IV Strong Point
    1   " " No. V   " "

On ascertaining that the 91st Brigade had been held up on our left, which was thus exposed, the officer commanding B Coy. asked for further help and 2 platoons of C Coy., who had been bombing "dug-outs" but had rejoined Hqrs. went sent forward and eventually occupied MAPLE TRENCH – D Coy. in reserve had followed B Coy. and detached one platoon to garrison Strong Point II, placing the remaining platoon in POMMIER TRENCH – This Coy. and part of Hqrs. came in for heavy shell fire and suffered severely. By about 10-15 a.m. all Strong Points in the first objective had been occupied and were being placed in a state of defence and the task allotted to the Battalion had been accomplished.

The two platoons of C and two of D Coys. who went over with the Royal Fusiliers and Bedfords worked through the 3 front lines of the enemy trenches on a set plan and carried out their work thoroughly & well. Three sections of D Coy. however suffered very heavily from machine gun fire and were practically wiped out.

Liason was well maintained between the battalion and the companies on its right and left.

All company commanders carried out their orders correctly and handled their companies with gallantry & skill. Platoons were well led both by officers and N.C.O.s.

Signalling was perhaps our weakest point - Runners and bearers worked splendidly.

2nd Lt. Price distinguished himself by the excellent and reliable information which he obtained.

Bn. Hqrs. was first established at PICCADILLY and afterwards moved to the front in BUND TRENCH about 100 yards W of the TRIANGLE.

The following casualties occurred on this day

    Officers wounded :-   Capt. Neville, Frank Septimus
                                     Lieut. Shankster, George
                                     2nd Lieut. Hamilton, Noel Crawford

    Other ranks :-   Killed 29, Wounded 123, Missing 4, Shell shocks, 1
             Total   3 Officers, Other Ranks 157

Copies of congratulatory messages received are attached   Appendix B

<u>Appendix B</u>

THE FOLLOWING MESSAGES ARE TO ALL CONCERNED

1. General CONGREVE wires please convey to all ranks my intense appreciation of their splendid fighting which has attained all asked of them and resulted in heavy losses to the enemy nearly 1000 prisoners have already passed through the cage aaa Ends.

2. General SIR H. RAWLINSON aaa Please ~~noe~~ convey to 18th. Div. my best congratulations and thanks for their dashing attack yesterday aaa They have done excellent work and I desire to thank them most heartily aaa.

3. General MAXSE to 18th. Div. aaa Well done its what I expected, now hold on to what you have gained so splendidly.

4. The COMMANDING OFFICER desired to congratulate the Regiment on the above complimentary messages from the Divisional, Corps and Army Commanders. At the same time he desired to thank all ranks for the splen-did way in which they carried out their role in the attack. A task in which most of them were required to face a heavy shell fire without the excitement of getting at close quarters with the enemy. This entails the highest courage and discipline which the Regiment most fully displayed.

       (sd) W.BARKHAM, Lieut. & Adjutant.
           6th. (S) Bn. Northamptonshire Regiment.

In the Field
1 - 7 - 16

I'm not cold but I'm finding it difficult to stop shaking now that I'm out of my bubble. I wish I could stop my head ringing; it feels like I'm in St. Katherine's belfry during bell practice. What have we just been through? I thought there weren't supposed to be anybody left alive after the pasting we gave em. The first few innocent seconds was instantaneously shattered as the

Bosche popped up like rabbits and starting to shoot at anything that moved, and there was a lot of movement to shoot at.

Lads falling, falling, falling, explosions everywhere, short chattering bursts from machine guns and bullets cracking past me forever or thudding as they connected with the ground or a body. Screams, screams, screams, blood curdling cries for help or the emptiness of the repeated unanswered question.

Whistles blowing, orders shouted above the screams, explosions, chatter, chatter, chatter... nothing in my mind... unconsciously looking for a safe haven... a transitory face belonging to the barked order penetrating the muffled cacophony of my mind.

Where to go, there... there... there? Zigzag, zigzag, get across the open ground; where's the next protection? Don't stop for anyone or anything.

They told us it would be a walk in the park; some bloody walk in the park...

July 2ⁿᵈ Consolidation of position was continued.

Casualties : Other Ranks – Killed 2, Wounded 30, Missing 5

Absolute carnage – there were dead, wounded and bits of people everywhere! Even when we tried to clean up, they shot at us. I thought, *nobody could have withstood what we threw at em.* Consolidate they ordered; how the hell do you consolidate total carnage and destruction?

I called it horror detail – the burial of what used to be fine young men. Every way you can think of destroying a person was about us. Shell shocked brains in another world, partly buried bodies in distorted and grotesque positions, a leg here, an arm there, fingers with no hands, heads missing or partly blown away, limbs without bodies, bodies without limbs, bodies without bodies, guts everywhere and blood, blood, blood...

The hardest part though was no body, just a disk, a piece of clothing, an item of personal equipment with a name or number on it.

Consolidate meant rebuild and bury; the rebuild was relatively easy, the horrific part was having to drive off the rats, search the carnage and devastation and retrieve whatever we could to try and identify the mutilated and rat eaten flesh.

In the right breast pocket, we would find their pay books, in the left, their wallets, around their necks, if they still had heads, their ID disks. We were instructed to tie the pay books and wallets together in a little bundle and after we had either buried them in a grave or just filled in the trench or shell hole where they lay, we were then to put a bayonet at the head of the corpse, tie the bundle to the top of the bayonet and place a tin helmet over the bayonet to shelter the bundle from the weather.

This was their burial, their cross, their end.

July 3rd A Coy. relieved the 7th Bedfordshire Rgt. in EMDEN TRENCH
 B Coy. relieved the 7th " " in BUND TRENCH and No. 11 Strong Point
 C and D remained in their old positions

What a difference a day makes, especially under the circumstances. I thought, *I must keep what I've just experienced at the back of my mind, don't think about it.* I smiled as I saw the 7th Beds coming to relieve us and I thought, *what a welcome sight – good luck lads and keep your heads down.*

July 4 The work of consolidation was continued
 Casualties :- Other Ranks :- Wounded 4

July 5 THE LOOP

" 6 The battalion moved into bivouacs during the evening to THE LOOP near BRONFAY FARM.

My guts are still burning and it's stopping me getting a full rest; a bite to eat should relieve the pain a bit so let's see if I can find a place to get comfortable.

Christ I'm tired and however much I try, I just can't get the last battle out of my mind. So many destroyed, killed and injured and for what? God knows what the count was but it must have been in the hundreds, if not thousands. Yes, we won this fight but at what cost? News from the other fronts said the lads followed orders and just walked in line and that they were mown down and ripped to pieces. There wasn't even any thought process in it; they just walked until they reached the enemy trench, *sheer bloody madness* I though. *Our tactics were far more successful, and I have to believe in them because I'm still in one piece. My Trudy would never understand the fear and carnage I've just been through – God, I hope she's never in a situation that the local people find themselves; poor buggers.*

This itching is getting through to me. I think I'll get some scoff and have a chat with the lads while I burn the lice from my clothes. It should take my mind off everything.

" 7 The C. In C. issued the following congratulatory message from H.M. The King :- "Please convey to the Army under your command my sincere congratulations on the results achieved in the recent fighting. I am proud of my troops, none could have fought more bravely".

Nice to know somebody thinks we did well and being the 8th, it's nice to be alive to celebrate Phyllis May's and my birthday today. I wonder what she's doing today; two years old, must be walking well by now and trying to talk her head off. God I miss my cuddles and play with the kids. Ah well, might as well celebrate my 35th with a cup of petrol tinted brew. Have a lovely day my child, love you.

BOIS DE TAILLES

" 9 The battalion moved during the evening into camp at BOIS DE TAILLES

Got news that Fred Atthews was killed yesterday, God rest his soul; another good man lost forever. I'm glad the news arrived after my birthday...

" 10 Maj. Gen. Maxse visited the camp -
" 11   Nil
" 12   Nil

MAICOURT

July 13 6:30 a.m.   The battalion paraded at 6:30 a.m. but did not reach MARICOURT till about 12 noon owing to being held up for a long period near BILLON WOOD. The battalion occupied various dug-outs in and around the ruins of the town, which was under rather heavy shell fire – Hqrs. in the cellar in the Chateau stables.

Up at an ungodly hour to parade – what sense is there in this after the carnage of the last couple of weeks? I still can't get the fear out of me; every explosion makes me duck and scares the shit out of me. What the hell am I going to be like at the end of the war if we have to keep going through that carnage and destruction?

Today, you would have been ten years old Lucy Jane; I wonder what your future would have looked like if you'd have lived? From what I've seen here, you're in the best and safest place but I miss you so, so much my child. Life's so cruel. Love you.

THE BATTLE OF BAZENTIN RIDGE AND CAPTURE OF TRONES WOOD

Appendix IV

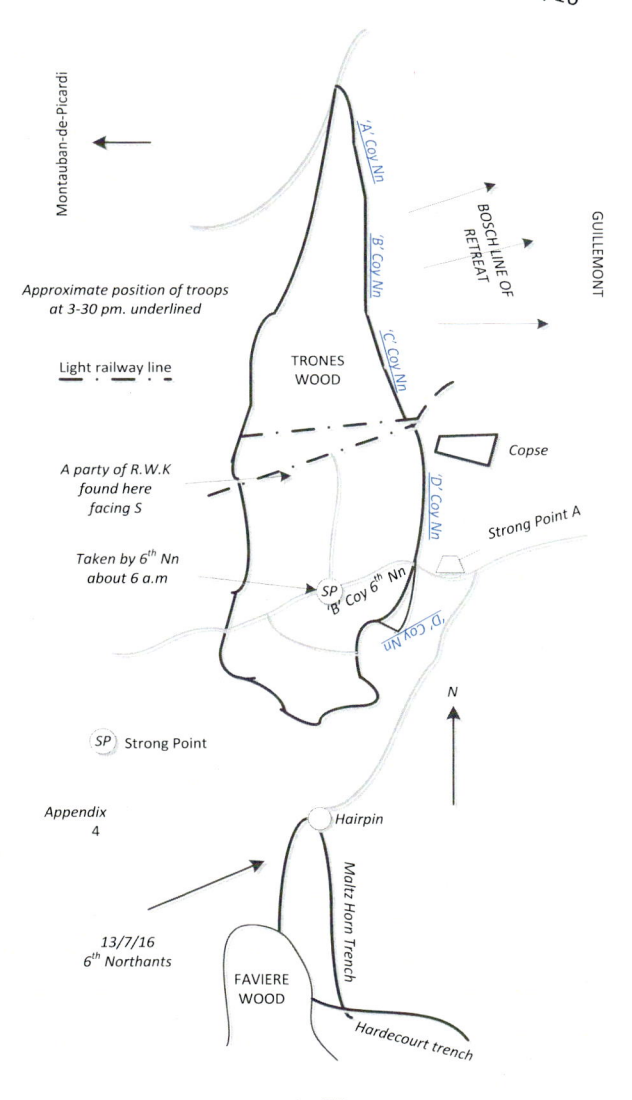

OPERATIONS IN TRONES WOOD 14/7/16

Montauban-de-Picardi

'A' Coy Nn
'B' Coy Nn
'C' Coy Nn

BOSCH LINE OF RETREAT

GUILLEMONT

Approximate position of troops at 3-30 pm. underlined

Light railway line

TRONES WOOD

Copse

A party of R.W.K found here facing S

'D' Coy Nn

Strong Point A

Taken by 6th Nn about 6 a.m

SP 'B' Coy 6th Nn

'D' Coy Nn

N

(SP) Strong Point

Appendix 4

Hairpin

Maltz Horn Trench

13/7/16
6th Northants

FAVIERE WOOD

Hardecourt trench

Operations resulting in the capture of TRONES WOOD

For Map & Sketch Map see Appendix 4 & 5
(Pages 80 & 81 of War Diary WO-95-2044-2_1)

14th   At 10-45 p.m. orders were received to send two companies (C & D were sent) to relieve two companies 12th Middlesex Rgt. in ~~DUBIN~~ DUBLIN TRENCH.

At 2-45 a.m. the remaining two companies (A & B) and Hqrs. were ordered to march to the SUNKEN ROAD, E. of BRIQUETRIE, where they would form up with C & D companies, who had been moved forward from DUBLIN TRENCH. At the same time Major Charrington received orders to report himself to the 54th Bde. Hqrs., where he received the following verbal instructions from the G.O.C.

That he was placed in command of the battalion for an attack on TRONES WOOD – Lt. Col. Maxwell V.C., D.S.O., C.S.I. being in command of the whole operation.

Our artillery barrage would lift from the wood at 4-30 a.m. The 7th R. W. Kents were holding a line from E to W across the Southern portion of the wood. The role of the 6th Northants would be that of supporting battalion to the 12th Middlesex, who would be in the front line.

The duties of the battalion were to clear up behind the front line and form a defensive flank on the Eastern edge of the wood. Maj. Charrington was to report himself to Lt. Col. Maxwell who would be found somewhere in the Southern edge of the wood." Col. Ripley was retained at 54th Bde. Hqrs. as liason officer.

Maj. Charrington left Bde. Hqrs. at 3-25 a.m. & arrived at BRIQUETRIE about 4-10 a.m. where he found Lt. Col. Maxwell, who informed him that he had been unable to collect all his battalion and had detailed the 6th Northants as the attacking line – Orders had been given to Major Clark and the battalion were then moving Eastwards long the SUNKEN ROAD to get into position for an advance on the Southern edge of TRONES WOOD. ~~From~~

From Major Clark, the following resumé of the orders he had issued was received.

"The battalion was to move forward to the line held by the 7th R.W. Kent Rgt. From there they were to clear the wood of the enemy to its extreme northern point. A & B Companies in the front line line – C Coy. in support, D. Coy. in reserve. Bn. Hqs. in centre of SUNKEN ROAD. There was no time to obtain any more detailed information as the two leading companies were already – 4-25 a.m – advancing across the open towards the Southern edge of the wood.

The advance took place over 1000 yards of open ground, which was smothered by an intense barrage of large calibre H.E. shells from the hostile artillery.

The companies advanced through this barrage with the greatest coolness & steadiness and suffered a good many casualties before reaching the wood.

Lt. & Adjt. Barkham and Bn. Hqrs. except 4 runners, were left in the SUNKEN ROAD and Major Charrington accompanied Lt. Col. Maxwell and Maj. Clark into the wood to get into touch with the O.C. 7th R. W. Kent Rgt. and ascertain the situation-

The Hqrs. of the 7th R.W.K was found in the shallow trench in the S.W. corner of the wood – From Lt. Col. Fiennes, commanding 7th R.W.K we learnt that portions of his battalion were holding a line near the light railway & that he had a detached post holding a Strong Point in the northern apex of the wood.

It turned out later that no men of the R.W.K were found anywhere north of the light railway line that runs E & W through centre of the wood. 2nd. Lt. Price, D Coy. & 2nd Lt. Walker C Coy. both reported finding R.W.K in a trench on edge of wood S. of Strong Point A. The latter reported three officers with this party, who said they were short of ammunition & requested reinforcements to be left with them. 2nd Lt Price reported that this party at first mistook ~~the~~ his men for the enemy & opened fire on them.

Captain Podmore reported that a party of R.W.K. were found lining the light railway running across centre of wood – They were facing south and also mistook his men for the enemy and opened fire on them.

	It was with the greatest difficulty and not until a compass had been produced that they could be persuaded that they were not facing northwards. No one in the battalion ever reported having found any of the R.W.K north of the line.
	In addition to the enemy's artillery barrage which was kept on the southern portion of the wood there were sounds of heavy rifle & machine gun fire from a point a little further in the interior. In the meantime, Lt.
A.M.	Col. Maxwell went back to the South edge of the wood to collect the 12th Middlesex which had not yet arrived.
4-45	Message was received from Major Clark that D Coy. was holding the trench running NE & S.W. towards Strong Point B. German bombers were holding Strong Point about 40 yards to their right – W. Kent officer reports that they are holding N end of wood –
	I sent a message to Major Clark that O.C. 7th R.W.K confirmed the report that they were holding N end of wood
5-10	Captain Podmore reported that his company were advancing N.E. and bombing up trench running from S.W. corner of the wood, and that he was in trench with portions of B & C Coys. on his right but not with the A Coy. He also reported that he was held up by Strong Point B and that he urgently required more bombs. Major Clark killed, Captain Shepherd wounded, & only about 100 men of his company left.
	Major Charrington only had one runner with him at the time, so collecting as many bombs as he could carry, he went forward to ascertain the situation & instructions were left for more bombs to be sent us as soon as possible and these were soon afterwards brought up by men of the Middlesex Rgt.
	Men of B & D Coys. were found creeping up to the Strong Point through the undergrowth, whilst those attempting to get round by the trench were held up owing to lack of bombs. Heavy rifle and machine gun fire was coming from the Strong Point – Captain Shepherd, although wounded in the shoulder was standing up in the open cheering on his men in the most gallant manner – On a fresh supply of bombs arriving the attach was pushed home, and the Strong

6-0	Point captured about 6-0 a.m. Many dead Germans were found at this spot –
	From this time onwards, owing to the impenetrable nature of the wood, heavy losses amongst officers and leaders units became mixed up and it was difficult to obtain a coherent idea of the situation.
8-05	Lt. Col. Maxwell proceeded to eastern edge of the wood to clear up situation and endeavour to reorganise units. He requested Major Charrington to remain where he was until his return.
9-15	Following message was received from Capt. Podmore (timed 9-0 a.m.) "Have secured all TRONES WOOD, except small T head containing about 6 men by Strong Point on GUILLEMONT ROAD. Also about 40 Germans in trench outside wood just S of same Strong Point. BUFFS are attacking with Stokes gun. We must have a Stokes gun if we are to take these two places. Am consolidating E. edge of TRONES WOOD." Above had since been confirmed in a letter from Capt. Podmore (wounded) in which he says :- "I sent Lt. Redhead to work N. through the wood. He did so with great success clearing the wood up the W. side up to the North point & then moving down again the E. side till he joined us by the Strong Point on the GUILLEMONT road."
9-02	2nd Lt. Price reported that D Coy. were now occupying main trench running from N. to S. through middle of wood. Enemy were clear of the wood on East & South but snipers still in evidence to the North.
9-25	2nd Lt. Redhead reported that his company were holding a position on E. edge of wood N. of Strong Point A. Enemy running away to the East being fired on by 12th Middlesex with machine guns.
	This was presumably from Strong Point A which had been captured by 12th Middlesex & 7th Buffs about 9 a.m. From this time till about 11:30 a.m. practically no information was received from the front but Lt. Col. Maxwell was on the spot re-organising units.
A.M.	Message received from 2nd Lt. Price, "Have taken over command of B Coy. Strength at present appears to be about 50. Am hanging on to our

11-30 — position running the East side of wood. Line very thin please try & get reinforcements up – Am unfortunately hit in the leg and cannot get along line very fast."

~~At this time an~~ – About the same time 2nd Lt. Walker arrived & asked for reinforcements for C. Coy. which had suffered many casualties & was also on Eastern edge of wood. An officer of 11th Royal Fusiliers, who were in support, had just reported to Maj. Charrington with one company, so he was requested to send one platoon to reinforce our Eastern flank, which was done. This platoon ~~were~~ was later established in Strong Point A. The other 3 platoons R.F. were being heavily shelled in the wood & were ordered to fall back to a trench about 400 yards in rear. The only shelter in the southern part of the wood which was under a continuous artillery barrage, being a shallow trench already choked with wounded.

" Approximate position of troops, as far as can be ascertained at this time is shown in sketch map. The trench shown running parallel to S.E. edge of wood was found by 2nd Lt. Walker to be occupied by 3 officers and a party of 7th R.W. Kent regiment about 6 a.m. They were in a somewhat exhausted condition and were relieved about 9 a.m.

Before this time the backbone of the ~~Defence~~ enemys' resistance had been broken by the capture of Strong Point A & B. The brunt of the fighting had been borne by 6th Northants, who had suffered severe casualties both in officers and men. The wood was now clear of the enemy, at any rate, except for snipers.

Lt. Col. Maxwell then organised a drive to clear the Northern half of snipers and break up any resistance still left.

Whilst this drive was in progress, the machine guns of 12th Middlesex & 7th Buffs. in Strong Point A and 2 Lewis guns of 6th Northants near the COPSE, were given excellent targets, as the enemy fled across the open towards GUILLEMONT and accounted for many enemy -

P.M.

1-30 — No news has been received at Adv. Report Centre in S. of TRONES WOOD of or from Lt. Co. Maxwell since 9:05 a.m. & it was thought that possibility he has become a casualty.

2-30	Lt. Col. Maxwell returned & gave Major Charrington orders to collect & reorganise the scattered units of the 6th Northants and as soon as they should be relieved by the 12th Middlesex on the Eastern edge of the wood, to take over the MALTZ HORN TRENCH from the 7th Buffs, keeping one Coy. in support in the South of TRONES WOOD.
3-30	Units were discovered, distributed approximately as shown in sketch.
5-30	12th Middlesex commenced relieving 6th Northants from the North. 6th Northants were formed up in wood to W. of the COPSE. After stragglers had been collected the battalion only mustered as follows:-

		Officers	Other Ranks
A Coy.	2nd Lt. Herries Smith		57
B Coy.	2nd Lt. Price (wounded in leg slightly)		69
C Coy.	2nd Lt. Walker		76
D Coy.	Capt. Podmore (slightly wounded)		45
	shrapnel in back)		247

Total of 3 unwounded officers, including Major Charrington, & 247 other ranks.

This was all that remained out of 17 regimental officers, and about 550 other ranks that had left the SUNKEN ROAD and entered TRONES WOOD a few hours previously – Lt. Newberry, the Medical Officer had

P.M.	also been killed, between TRONES and BERNAFAY WOOD, whilst performing his duties in the most gallant manner.
6-0	The battalion were then moved into the MALTZ HORN TRENCH, except B Coy. under 2nd Lt. Price, who were left in support in the trench previously occupied by the 7th R.W. Kents.

On the weak state of the battalion being explained to Lt. Col. Ransome, Commdg. 7th Buffs. & to 54th Bde. Hqrs. it was arranged that the 7th Buffs should continue to hold the MALTZ HORN line for the night, the 6th Northants remaining in support in the same trenches in which there was plenty of spare room.

Casualties during the day had been as follows :-

∅ since reported "killed"

Officers killed – (5)	Officers wounded – (9)	Other Ranks
Major Clark G.M. C Coy	Capt. Shreiner - O.D. A Coy	Killed - 30
2nd Lt. Lys F.G.B C "	" Shepperd - S.F. B "	Wounded - 198
" Farrell R D "	Lt. Arnold - J.F. D "	Missing - 35
" Hamilton N.C B "	∅ " Wilcox - F.A.C A "	Shell shocked 7
Lt. Newberry R.F.T	2nd Lt. Fawkes - R.B. D "	270
(R.A.M.C.)	" Redhead - A.H. D "	
Missing (1)	" Greenwood - J B "	Officers - 15
∅ 2nd Lt. Woulfe C.L. A Coy.	" Price - T.R D "	
	Capt. Podmore - H D "	

During the night 14/15 July, the following further casualties were reported:-

Other Ranks

Killed - 2 - Wounded - 9 - Missing 2 - Shell shock 5 - Total 18

Making grand total of Officers -   15

Other Ranks   288

All Ranks   303

Considering the disadvantageous circumstances under which the attack was carried out, the operation, resulting in the complete capture and occupation of TRONES WOOD, the capture of which had been attempted and at any rate partially failed on at least three previous occasions, ~~may~~ reflects the greatest credit on all concerned –

The battalion was thrown into the wood in so much haste, that it was impossible to explore in any detail the plan of attack.

After passing through an extremely severe artillery barrage across 1,000 yards of open country, the battalion was met, before it had proceeded more than about 150 yards into the wood by heavy machine gun & rifle fire –

Without the slightest hesitation the attack was immediately launched & pushed home with the greatest vigour. It was inevitable that in the ensuing fighting units should become mixed up & to a certain extent lose direction, especially in the *attack, which had been launched, as this one had, without the opportunity for the least preparation.*

There is no doubt that the backbone of the ~~attack~~ resistance in the centre of the wood, was broken entirely by the vigorous initiative taken by the company commanders & other subordinate leaders – It was during the early stages that most of the casualties occurred amongst the officers of the battalion.

Major Clark, Captains Shreiner, Shepherd & Podmore ~~were~~ all became casualties ~~at~~ very soon after commencement of the attack. The former being killed whilst gallantly reconnoitring in the front of his Company. Many subaltern officers were also put out of action at this period.

Under these circumstances, it can scarcely be wondered at, that after the fight had been proceeding for about 3 hours, a considerable degree of disorganisation had resulted – A contributory cause was the impenetrableness of the wood, which had been rendered much worse by the heavy artillery bombardment to which it had been subjected from our own & enemy guns, which had laid trees flat in every direction, causing an impassable network of trunks and branches.

I was in my bubble again, focused on protection in whatever form, trying to work out the direction of the chatter, half listening for shouted orders from transitory faces, there's more thuds than cracking bullets. Stumbling past mates crying out for help as I force through a half dead wall of undergrowth.

It was an assault course, climbing over and ducking under broken trees, crawling on my stomach and dodging the bullets between cover. The guys kept falling, falling... there wasn't a green leaf that wouldn't join the rest in death because, like us, they were clinging to broken branches that were clinging to broken trunks that were clinging to broken earth; utter madness.

We couldn't dig-in through the roots, every trunk had at least 2 men behind it and lying down was no better because the bullets kept cracking past a few inches above the ground.

It was unbelievably hard but we captured the southern wood strong point before we had time for a breather. The Bosche put up a hell of a fight. I was thinking, *OK, seems like I'm in one piece, no blood and everything looks in order. Right, let's go.*

We're making ground through and I can see daylight on either side of the wood so we must be getting closer to our top of the wood objective.

I heard a crack and a thud and looking over my shoulder I saw, in slow motion, my mate's head explode and his totally limp body falling to the ground. My bubble evaporated and I was totally engulfed in fear and confusion and I instinctively dropped to the ground. A crack and the bubble engulfed me again, I got up and started looking for my next protection.

A face appeared in my head and the voice ordered us to take up a position on the right to the east of the wood where the Bosche were retreating. Was it a subconscious act of revenge as I thought, *the Bosche are running over open fields, easy targets, let's see if I can get a few.*

Crack, crack, crack - *what?! What the hell?! Where the hell are those coming from?! They're our own.* A voice, that I couldn't connect with a face, is shouting for a messenger to deliver a letter.

Keep down Bob until they work out that we're on the same side and stop shooting at us. Surely, it can't get worse than this!

When the Bosche were too far away to be easy targets, my bubble started expanding. I felt extremely tired and lonely and without sense. Although I was surrounded by my mates, I felt isolated and I thought, *what to do, what to do...*

After a couple of hours consolidation, my mind started to reflect, *Trones Wood?! Trones Wood?! Call this a wood?! It's just impenetrable undergrowth, devastated trees and corpses!*

The 7th Queens and Buffs took it hard but they ended up capturing nothing. What the hell happened to the 12th Middlesex?! We were supposed to be in Reserve and we ended in the front line without any preparation.

After the 1st July, I thought I knew what hell was but today, attacking through swarms of angry bullets and endless explosions over totally open uphill ground towards a wood that hides everything, I have just experienced a deeper level of hell.

MALTZE HORN TRENCH

15th   Hqrs. at N. end of HAIRPIN.
Reinforcements began to arrive. 2nd Lt. Chatham arrived ~~to~~ on previous evening.
Lt. Batty early in morning. Lt. & Adjt. Barkham arrived from SUNKEN ROAD. About 8 a.m. Capt. Evans, Lt. Eldridge & 2nd Lt. Keyes & Gillot arrived.
This allowed Capt. Podmore & 2nd Lt. Price, both of whom had been wounded on previous day & refused to leave their companies, to be relieved 2nd Lt. ~~Hyam~~ Higham also arrived with 60 other ranks, but as the ~~7th~~ Buffs were still holding the MALTZ HORN TRENCH, these were sent back to FAVIERRE TRENCH until required in front line –

15th   During the evening orders arrived from 54th Bde. Hqrs. for reconstruction of the line holding MALTZ HORN TRENCH – At this time B Coy. had already proceeded under orders from Lt. Col. Maxwell from their support trench in the S.E. edge of TRONES WOOD to the northern point of the wood

I need a rest from this wood. More lads killed and injured. If this isn't hell on earth then I don't know what is. Everything is destroyed and the destroyed is piled on top of the destroyed. My guts hurt, my head's ringing like crazy, my bloody feet hurt, I stink, the bloody lice are eating me alive as are the bloody rats!

I desperately need a rest and a decent brew. Irchester must be wonderful now basking in the summer sun with Trudy and the kids holding buttercups under their chins and making daisy chains in the green fields behind St. Katharine's

    – A Coy. was employed transferring bombs & ammunition from TRONES WOOD to a dump in STRONG POINT A - C Coy. was collecting picks & shovels & carrying them to the same places & 2 ~~Coy~~ platoons of D Coy. were unloading mules in the valley S. of STRONG POINT A.

16th   Hqrs. had been moved during afternoon from HAIRPIN to a point 1000 yards further N. in MALTZ HORN TRENCH.

The line allotted to the battalion was from the South point of the road in MALTZ HORN TRENCH near point 6550 in S. 30-C to an including the COPSE in almost centre of Eastern edge of TRONES WOOD. Companies were distributed as follows:- B Coy. from right of our line to Strong Point A exclusive; C Coy. in Strong Point A; D Coy. from Strong Point A exclusive to northern edge of the COPSE inclusive; A coy. in support in trench on S.E. edge of TRONES WOOD.

Bn. Hqrs. in northern part of 7th Buffs. line until accommodation could be arranged in Strong Point A.

The relief was completed & line taken over about 5 a.m.

During afternoon, orders were received from Bde. Hqrs. to occupy ARROW HEAD COPSE.

A patrol was at once despatched there to reconnoitre, saw no signs of enemy but was fired on by our own artillery - Artillery were requested not to fire anymore & at 10:30 p.m. ARROW HEAD COPSE was occupied by a detachment of 10 men & a Lewis gun, without opposition – At the same time a patrol proceeded about 300 yards along the trench which runs eastwards from Strong Point A in direction of GUILLEMONT & met with no signs of the enemy –

I'm really, really tired and it's nice to hear at last that we're being relieved to live another day.

17   The battalion was relieved by 3 companies, 15th Sherwood Foresters (Bantams)

The relief was completed by 4-30 a.m.

The battalion arrived at COPSE D.   S. of MARICOURT about 6-45 a.m. & went into dug-outs.

The account of above operations is unavoidably incomplete & possibly in some particulars inaccurate – it is always difficult to follow the course of events in an operation of this nature, especially so in the present case, when there are only two officers remaining, both very junior, who took part in the attack, from whom any first hand information can be obtained∅ –

∅more information has since been obtained by letter from wounded officers

The whole battalion, both officers, N.C.O.s & men behaved with the greatest gallantry. With regards to the officers, the casualty list speaks for itself.

The medical staff and stretcher bearers, personally directed by their Medical Officer Lt. R. F. T. Newberry R.A.M.C carried out their duties with the greatest devotion and suffered many casualties –

It is impossible to speak too highly of the self sacrifice & fearlessness of Lt. Newberry, who lost his life whilst carrying out his duties to the utmost of his abilities –

The Rev. A.E. Bennet also showed bravery of the highest order in his administration to & assistance to the wounded under heavy shell fire.

The transport & supply arrangements under Lt. Beasley & Lt. Fowler were carried out, often in positions of considerable danger with the greatest energy and zeal.

Runners, as usual performed their hazardous & exhausting duties with great courage and devotion to duty.

The report cannot close without a tribute to the memory of Major Clark, who was killed in action early on the 14th July –

This officer by his soldierly qualities, his coolness under fire & the interest he always took in the welfare of his men, endeared himself to all ranks. His loss will be keenly felt & his place hard to refill. The names of those who have been brought to the notice for special acts of gallantry & devotion to duty have been forwarded to the proper quarter.

COPSE D   S of MARICOURT

17th (cont)   The battalion rested after ~~98 hours with~~ *having had* scarcely any sleep for 98 hours
The following was published in Regimental orders.
"The G.O.C. in C has under special authority granted by H.M The King awarded the "Military Cross" of 1st July 1916 to 3/11054   R.S.M Fulcher F."

Nice to hear of the award to the RSM but I'm quite happy just being awarded a rest. Looking back at the feeling of freedom during our marches through the open fields, I feel like a bloody idiot now because I've realised that the openness just makes me an easy target.

BOIS DE TAILLES

18th The battalion marched from COPSE D at 8 p.m. and arrived at ~~camp~~ camp in BOIS DE TAILLES about midnight – A draft of 300 N.C.Os & men joined the battalion.

After days of fighting and working with virtually no sleep, they march us for hours to a camp. At least we're marching away from the front line so there's a big incentive to keep up.

19th C.O. inspected the battalion

News is that we're in for a train ride so it must be a long way. At least the weather's nice and it takes my mind off the bloody ringing in my head. The scoff's given my guts a rest as well so life's not too bad.

21st The battalion paraded at 1-30 p.m. & marched to EDGE HILL STATION arriving about 3-45 p.m. Train supposed to leave at 4 p.m. did not depart with the battalion until 10-30 p.m.

CITERNES

22nd Battalion arrived at LONGPRES-les-Corps-Saints at 6-30 a.m. by train, thence by train to WIRY au-MONT & thence marched about 1½ miles to billets at CITERNES arriving about 9-45 a.m.

WALLON CAPPEL

23rd Battalion paraded at 5 a.m. and marched back to LONGPRES arriving at 8-45 a.m., entrained at 9-45 a.m. proceeded via ETAPLES & ST. OMAER and arrived at ARQUES at 5 p.m. Left ARQUES at 7-30 p.m. and marched to WALLON CAPPEL ~~arriving~~ (almost 9 miles) arriving at 11-0 p.m. Battalion billeted in various farm houses spread out over about 1½ miles.

That was a nice long restful train journey, apart from losing a few quid at cards, and the march at the end also got the legs moving again. We've been told that we're travelled about a hundred and twenty odd miles due North of Albert.

24th   Battalion rested

    This is another world, just like the first little village we stayed at when I first arrived in France; so peaceful and quiet, apart from the intermittent ringing in my head. I don't know what I expected really but France and these little villages are a lot like Northamptonshire. Whoever made the decision to send us here for a rest, thank you. A couple of letters from Trudy as well as a Red Cross Parcel, so life's not all that bad hey Bob?

25th   Work on reorganization of battalion

    No rest for the wicked but I must say, a nice place and lovely weather to do it in. With all this activity of reorganisation I think, they're thinking, that we need to be kept from thinking. Just heard that William Reynolds from the village was killed the day before yesterday; poor bugger. I don't need to keep getting these reports but then again, I do. I need to keep the lovely pictures of Irchester and Astcote in my mind and any news, be it good or bad takes me back to Trudy, the kids and the good times.

26th   The battalion was inspected by the Divisional Commander at 11-30 a.m.

27th   Weather very hot. Company parades – Instruction in bombing – Lewis gun – drill etc.

    The ringing in my head seems to be constant now and I'm not the only one with the problem. Apparently it's from all the bomb blasts, bullet cracks, high pitched Officer's whistles and people screaming but at least it's not loud enough to bother me as much as the lice. I've noticed the ringing gets louder when I'm worried and when I'm concentrating on something it goes away. I hope that when all this is over, it'll stop altogether.

BAILLEUL

    Here we go again, march, march, bloody march but I suppose we have to look on the bright side, at least we're not being shot at. My guts are still playing up and it looks like a lot more of the lads are feeling the same. I'm not sure where the cooks came from but the scoff didn't taste right; perhaps the hot weather's turning the meat.

28th   Battalion paraded at 9 a.m. & marched with rest of 54th Inf. Bde. to BAILLEUL.

Owing to heat & an epidemic of diarrhoea which had broken out yesterday, many men, especially of the last draft fell out on the line of march.

Arrived at billets on BAILLEUL – ST. JANS CAPPEL road about 2-30 p.m.

29	2nd Lt. H.C. OSBORNE joined the battalion & was posted to C Coy.
30	Company parades. Bombing – Lewis gun – Bayonet fighting – Drill
31	instruction

G Ripley   Colonel
Commdg. 6th (S) Bn. Northamptonshire Regt.

1916
August
N.W. of BAILLEUL

1st Company Training
2nd Lt. A. BATES joined the battalion on 31-7-16 and was posted to D Coy.

2nd Lecture on Trench Warfare – Instruction in bombing & Lewis Gun. Coy. drill and bayonet fighting

My stomach's settled down and the general diarrhoea seems to have cleared up. Looking forward a game of footy tomorrow; must get the lads together and decide who's going to be in the team.

3rd Battalion route march. Battalion sports in afternoon

Ha, I enjoyed that, good fun and a bit of a laugh. Nothing like a good laugh and knockabout with a ball and beating the other Coys just added to the pleasure. More good news, a bath tomorrow and I've also got a letter from Trudy. She says everybody's well and the people of the village are mucking in to make the best of the circumstances. Life's good; time for a brew and write a letter home.

4th Lecture and instruction in gas helmets by Divl. Gas Expert. Baths at BAILLEUL.

I feel a lot better after a bit of delousing and a bath and judging by the larking about, the lad's feel the same way too.

2nd Lieut. H.W. STONE joined the battalion on the 2nd inst. & was posted to B Coy. Lieut. C.G. KEMP (R.A.M.C.) appointed M.O. vice Capt. D. MACFARLANE (R.A.M.C.).

RUE MARLE ARMENTIERES

5th The Battalion marched from BAILLEUL at 5.15 p.m. and marched to RUE MARLE ARMENTIERES, where it arrived about 10 p.m. & went into billets.

Ah well, the rest was nice, not looking forward to tomorrow. Guts playing up again and the ringing in my head is louder again.

6th The Battalion took over various Strong Points in the 'subsidiary line", to be occupied in case of emergency.

7th to 10th   Training in bombing, Lewis gun, wiring, rapid loading & firing, rifle exercises.

After what we've been through, I would've thought we wouldn't need any more training but I suppose it keeps the mind occupied.

10th   C.O. 2nd in-command and Adjutant inspected left sector of 54th Brigade trench line.

11th   The Battalion left RUE MARLE by platoons at 7-30 a.m. and formed up at BAC ST. MAUR; left there at 9-30 a.m. and marched to camp ~~at~~ near LA MOTTE, arriving about 8-15 p.m. Distance about 17 miles. A very hot & fatiguing march.

Well, that wasn't nice; mad dogs and Englishmen tactics.

CAMP near LA MOTTE-au-Bois

~~8th~~   The following officers joined the battalion on the 8th inst. & were posted as follows :-
2nd Lt. W.H. GODDARD to B Coy. 2nd Lt. BAILEY to C Coy.
One man was killed & one man wounded by shell fire in RUE MARLE on 9th inst.

12th to 13th   Morning & afternoon. Practice in wood fighting in BOIS DES VACHES by platoons. Night practice by the battalion.
Practice in the attack on a wood in the BOIS DES VACHES. Inspected by Lt. Gen. Godley Commdg. 2nd ANZAC & G.O.C. 54th Inf. Bde.
Night practice, finding way through wood by ~~companies~~ platoons.

This wood fighting practice is interesting in that the trees are fully intact and upright but in the front line, they're broken to pieces, at all angles, mostly horizontal, and on top of each other.

14th   Morning. Battalion practice attack in wood.
Afternoon. Inspection of kits, arms & accoutrements

I must admit, these practice attacks are good fun because there's no explosions and nobody's shooting back at us.

RUE MARLE

15th   Battalion left camp near LA MOTTE-au-Bois in motor busses & lorries at 5-30 a.m. for ERQUINGHAM; marched from there & arrived in old billets at RUE MARLE about 8-15 a.m.   ♪ *There's no place like home...* ♪

B.2
Sector
II Army

Aug 16th The Battalion relieved the 7th Bedford Regt. in B.2 sector - The relief was carried out rapidly & without incident and was completed by 10-30 p.m. Coys were distributed as follows :- B Coy on right, A Coy in centre, C Coy on left of the line. D Coy in reserve near "The Orchard".

Orders for Relief see Appendix 6

Here we go again, back in the front line and more building work to do. The rest was good while it lasted and my guts are feeling much better. I wonder what Trudy and the kids are doing today.

SECRET.   Appendix 6
                    OPERATION ORDERS No.1.
                       By Colonel G.E. Ripley
              Commdg. 6th (S) Bn. Northamptonshire Regiment   15. 8. 16
1. INTENTION.   Ref. map Sheet 36 N.W. Edition 6B 1/20,000
            The 6th (S) Bn. Northants Regt will relieve the 7th Beds Rgt
   in B.2 Sector on the night 16th/17th Aug.1916

2. ORDER AND TIME OF RELIEF.
              "C" Coy will parade in time so that its leading platoon
   arrives at the Level Crossing LA CHAPPELLE ARMENTIARES I.8. Central
   at 9.15 p.m. and will relieve "C" Coy 7th Bn. Beds. Regt in the Left
   Sub-sector.
         "A" Coy will parade in time so that its leading platoonx
   arrives at the Level crossing LA CHAPPELLE ARMENTIARES I.8. Central
   at 9.35 p.m. and will relieve "B" Coy 7th Bn. Beds. Regt in the Centre
   Sub-sector.
         "B" Coy will parade in time so that its leading platoon
   arrives at xxx I.14.d.4.8. at 9.20 p.m. and will relieve "A" Coy
   7th Beds in the Right sub-sector.
         "D" Coy will parade in time so that its leading platoon
   arrives at I.14.d.4.8. at 9.40 p.m. and will relieve "D" Coy 7th Beds.
   in reserve at the ORCHARD.
   LEWIS GUNNERS, SIGNALLERS, SNIPERS, will parade in time so that the
   first named arrives at LA CHAPPELLE ARMENTIARES I.8.Central at 5 p.m.
   and the others at 15 minutes interval.
                Bn.H.Qrs will parade at 8.15 p.m.

3. INTERVAL. Platoons will move to their positions at 5 minutes
   interval and will march off with Right of the Coy leading i.e.
   "A" Coy No.1 platoon.

4. GUIDES.   Guides will meet each platoon at the above times and
   places stated.

5. MESS CART. The Mess Cart will call at Coy Messes at the following
   times :-
   "A" Coy, 8.30 p.m., H.Qrs. 8.40 p.m. "B" Coy, 8.50 p.m.
   "C" Coy, 8.55 p.m., "D" Coy 9 p.m.

6. <u>OFFICERS' KITS</u>. A limbered wagon will call at Coys for Officers' kits, commencing at "A" Coy at 8.30 p.m.

7. <u>TRENCH STORES</u>. Os. C. Coys wil forward a list to Bn.H.Qrs of all Trench Stores taken over.

8. <u>COOKING</u>. All cooking will be done in the Trenches the greatest care being taken that no unnecessary smoke is made from the kitchens.

9. <u>WATER</u>. Water can be obtained from the wells at CHARDS FARM and the ORCHARD.

10 <u>RATION DUMP</u>.
        The rations will be dumped at the Northern end of WINE AVENUE.

11 <u>COMPLETION OF RELIEF</u>.
    Os.C.Coys will report in writing to Bn.H.Qrs I.14.c.99 when they have completed the Relief.

              (Sgd) W.Barkham, Lieut & Adjt.
           6th (S) Bn. Northamptonshire Regiment

12 <u>OFFICERS' KITS</u>.
    Officers kits not required in the trenches will be collected at 3 p.m. today.

18th The following three officers joined the Battalion & were posted as follows :-
  2nd Lt. R.A. WEBB   -   D Coy
   "   " H.P. FREND   -   A Coy
   "   " L. NENDICK   -   B Coy

News arrived that Arthur Freeman was killed yesterday, may he rest in peace. I wonder where he's buried, that is, if they found much of him to bury?

19th to 22nd Nothing of importance occurred – A considerable amount of work done in rebuilding traverses & parapets & putting up wire in front of our front & support line trenches – Several officers patrols went out each night to examine ground in "No man's land" & also in order to train young officers. Enemy appeared very nervous in Sectors on our right, especially on night of 19th/20th. On night of 22/23, enemy put a few large trench mortar shells into left of our line but did scarcely any damage. Out artillery retaliated with 144 rounds 18 lb on his front line trenches causing casualties in one of his working parties. The weather was fine on the whole, though a little rain fell on the 18th & 19th.

This bloody tit-for-tat is getting on my nerves. Why don't they just keep quiet until we have to fight for real? I must admit, I'm not as jumpy as I used to be; must be getting used to it. I'm getting the impression that things are not working out well because we don't seem to be making or losing any ground.

News just arrived that another lad from the village, Fred Partridge was killed on the 20th, God rest his soul.

23rd During night on 23rd/24th the Battalion was relieved by 20th Bn. Northumberland Fusiliers – The relief was not completed till 11-55 p.m.   *Orders for Relief see Appendix 6A*

Total casualties during 8 days in trenches 4 O.Rs. wounded.

Appendix 6A   *WAR DIARY*

S E C R E T.   OPERATION ORDERS   No.2.

by Colonel G.E. Ripley   22. 8. 16

Commanding 6th (S) Bn. Northamptonshire Regiment.

Reference Map France, 1/40,000 Sheet 36.

1. <u>INTENTION</u>.

    The 6th (S) Bn. Northants Regt will be relieved by 20th Bn. Northumberland Fusiliers in B.2 Sub-section on the night 23rd/24th inst.

2. <u>TIME</u>.

    The hour of commencement of relief will be about 9 pm. The first platoon of 20th Northumberland Fusiliers will pass the level crossing I.8 Central at LA CHAPPELLE d'ARMENTIARES at 8.45 p.m.

3. <u>GUIDES</u>.

    One guide per platoon and one from Headquarters will report to the Adjutant at Bn.Hd.Qrs at 7.30 p.m. on the evening of the 23rd inst.

    O.C. "D" Coy will detail one officer to take charge of this party of guides. He will report at Bn.H.Qrs at 7.30 p.m. 23rd inst.

    Os.C.Coys will be responsible that each guide thoroughly understands the nearest way to lead the incoming platoons to the trenches.

4. <u>ORDERS OF RELIEF</u>.

    1st. "B" Coy, Right Sub-s.   2nd "A" Coy Centre Sub-s.
    3rd "C" "   Left " "   4th "D"   "   Res. ORCHARD.
    5th Headquarters.

5. <u>SPECIALISTS</u>. (Lewis Gunners, Snipers, Signallers etc.)

    Will be relieved about 2.30 p.m.

6. <u>ADVANCED PARTIES – 20th NORTHUMBERLAND FUSILIERS</u>.

    Advanced parties of the relieving battalion to take over Trench Stores will be at the level crossing I.8. Central at 5 p.m. One Guide per coy to be detailed.

7. TRENCH STORES.
Three Trench Stores Lists per Coy are issued herewith. All three will be made out by Coys and signed by the Officers who take over and hand over and will be distributed as follows :- One to Adjutant immediately on completion of relief, One handed to the Officer taking over and the other retained by Officer handing over.

All Battalion property will be taken out of the trenches such as Verey Pistols, Wire cutters, Wiring gloves etc. Maps, plans, aeroplane photographs and trench log-books will be handed over on relief.

8. COMPLETION OF RELIEF.
On completion of relief the 6th (S) Bn. Northants Regt will proceed by platoons to ERQUINCHEM via CHAPPELLE d'ARMENTYERES - RUE MARLE-EMERGENCY ROAD A.3. (near old Bn.H.Qrs).

9. KITS.
All Stores, Officers' kits, cooking utensils etc. will be dumped at the Coy ration Dumps by 7 p.m. the 23rd inst ready for loading. Each Coy and Bn.H.Qrs will detail a loading party of 1 N.C.O. and two men to load the limbers. These parties will travel with the kits.

All spare kit that is not required should be sent down by the Ration limber tonight, 22nd inst.

10. BILLETING PARTY.
2nd Lieut Walker and one senior N.C.O of each Coy will parade in time so that they arrive at ERQUINGHAM CHURCH **xx xxxx xxxxxxxxxxxxx by 2 p.m. to take over billets,** to report to the Adjutant before marching off.

The Sergt. Cook and one cook per Company will be sent forward to prepare hot tea for the men when they arrive in billets. The necessary cooking utensils will be sent down tonight the 22nd inst.

11. TRANSPORT.
O.C. Transport will arrange for one limber per Coy and one for Headquarters to be at the Coy Ration Dumps at 8.45 p.m. the 23rd inst. The First Line Transport will remain it its **xxxx**

present position until the Brigade marches out of ERQUINGHEM.

12. REPORT.
Os.C.Coys will report in the following manner xx on completion of relief (by phone) :-
"D" Coy 1010, meaning "D" Coy relieved at 10.10 p.m.

13. CLEANLINESS OF TRENCHES AND LINES.
Os.C.Coys are reminded that their cookhouse, latrines and trenches are handed over thoroughly clean.

(Sgd) W.Barkham, Lieut & Adjt.
6th (S) Bn. Northamptonshire Regiment.

ERQUINGHAM Erquinghem Lys

24th   The Battalion marched by platoons from B.2 Sub sectors & ~~bivouack billet~~ went into billets, the last platoon arriving in billets about 2 a.m.

This is a great day to celebrate our Alfred's birthday so, Happy Birthday Alfred, 15 years old. Time flies and I wish I could be there to see you developing into a young man. Leave the girls alone and stay out of the haystacks with them. Good luck for the future my son; I hope I'll be home soon to share in your wonderful teenage years. Love you so much my boy.

25th   Marched to ERQUINGHAM at 5 p.m. Arrived at BAILLEUL Station at 8 p.m. Left by train at 10-30 p.m.

I love these train journeys away from the front line. The moment I set my foot on the coach step, I feel a weight being lifted off my shoulders. The only thing that would make it more enjoyable is if I had a glass of beer in me mitt.

BAILLEUL AUX-CORNAILLES

Aug 26   Arrived at ST POL Station about 3 a.m. Marched at 4-15 a.m. arriving at BAILLEUL AUX-CORNAILLES about 7 a.m. & went into billets.
           C.O. & 2nd-in-Command attended a Bde. Conference at ORLENCOURT at 2 p.m.

27 to 30th } Company & Batallion training, in the MONCHY BRETON training area and near billets.
C.O. 2nd-in-command & Adjt Bde. Conference at Bde. Hqrs.

31st   Brigade training scheme in the attach. *Attachment was not provided in the War diary*

                                        S.H. Charrington Maj.
                         Commanding 6th (S) Bn. Northamptonshire Rgt.

BAILLEUL AUX CORNAILLES

Sept. 1st In morning Tactical training in MONCHY BRETON training area.
In afternoon Coy training in bayonet, bombing, physical training, rapid loading. Instruction & lecture on bayonet fighting & physical training by expert.

2nd All Coys attended baths at TINQUES.

Here I am, sitting in a bath and feeling a bit down because today is the 5th anniversary of our Eric's death. Still miss you son and I hope heaven is nice for you. Love you son.

C.O. & Capt. Evans departed to England on leave.

3rd Church Parade at 11.30 a.m. Lt MARGOLIOUTH departed to England on leave.

I'm not terribly religious but these church parades do make me feel a bit better. It must be because it gives us time to be quiet and think about those that are not, and will never be, with us again. Love you our Eric.

4th Brigade Tactical Scheme – Practice in attack on woods & rearguard action in MONCHY BRETON training area. Demonstration in constructing "dug-outs" & intensive digging.   1st & 2nd prizes in Intensive Digging Competition won by No. 11 Platoon, C. Coy.
1 Platoon from each Battalion in the Brigade competing.

They didn't win, we just didn't see the need to overexert ourselves. Another lad from the village won't be going home; William Joyce was reported killed yesterday.

5th In morning : training near billets under Coy Commanders
In afternoon : bombing & rapid firing on rifle range in training area.

6th In morning practice in intensive digging & following an artillery barrage on training area.

Not sure I like this idea of following a barrage. Too close for comfort for my liking.

C.O. Adjt. & O.C. A Coys attended demonstration in construction of tunelled dug-outs in afternoon.

Training, training, training but then again, I suppose it does keep us out of mischief.

85

7th   Battalion paraded at 3 a.m. and carried out tactical scheme in forming up in the dark & an attack on a platoon at dawn.

Forming up in the dark now, attacking a platoon and following a barrage; what's going on? These must be new tactics because the others certainly didn't bloody work. Ah, I see the combinations now. I see what's on their minds – have a go at em before they've had breakfast.

         In afternoon, practice in following artillery barrage & construction of tunnelled dug-outs on training area.

8th   In morning - (ditto)

         In afternoon - Rapid firing on rifle range in A.1. Area

BUNEVILLE

9th   The battalion marched from BAILLEUL AUX CORNAILLES with the rest of the 54th Inf.Bde. at 9-30 a.m. and arrived at BUNEVILLE at 12 noon and went into billets.

On our way back south towards Albert again. Still, a few days of marching through the open countryside in September is always a nice way to relax.

SUS ST LEGER

10th   The battalion left BUNEVILLE at 10-30 a.m. and marched with the 54th Inf. Bde. to SUS ST. LEGER, arriving at 1-45 p.m. Colonel Ripley and Capt. Evans returned from leave about 10-30 p.m.

ARQUÈVES

11th   The battalion left SUS ST LEGER and marched with 54th Inf. Bde. At 7-30 a.m. to HALLOY arriving there at 11 a.m. At 12 noon the battalion, the 12th Middlesex Rgt & 54th T.M. battery left in busses & motor lorries for ARQUÈVES arriving at 1-45 p.m. & went into billets. The battalion joined the II Corps of the Reserve Army and has during last 3½ months been in every Army except the 1st. During the march from BAILLEUL AUX CORNAILLES only one man fell out.

Mmmmmm, I wonder who's been awarded the medals this time? Our Trudy would be over the moon if I got one. Then again, perhaps she wouldn't because it means I've been in the thick of it and putting our future life at risk. Better I just do my bit and keep a low profile rather than make her fret.

On 10th inst. fourteen N.C.O.s & men of the battalion were awarded the Military Medal for acts of gallantry performed on the 1st & 14th July 1916.

See Appendix 13

Sept.
ARQUÈVES

12th The C.O. & 2nd in-Command viewed the lines around THIEPVAL from various Observation Posts. Coy Training in bayonet fighting, rapid loading, physical training, advancing behind barrage etc. 2nd Lt. Margoliouth returned from leave

13th Coy training, same as yesterday. 2nd Lt. Margoliouth returned from leave.

14th Battalion route march, less 1 platoon per company, who practiced construction of tunnelled dug-outs.

Not very pretty around here. It's seen a lot of action and most of the structures are just rubble. I can't even picture what it must have looked like.

2nd Lt. W. C. CLOSE joined the battalion on 12th inst & was posted to D. Coy.

A draft of 10 N.C.O.s & men joined the battalion.

15th Coy training. Most of the battalion attended baths at near VAUCHELLES-les-Authie.

Ah, nice, clean and fresh again; pity about having to put on some of my dirty clothes again but what the heck, at least I feel better.

16th Battalion tactical scheme (outposts) in morning. In afternoon the C.O. presents the ribbon of the MILITARY MEDAL to the N.C.O.s & men to whom the Medal had been awarded. Appendix 13

6th (S) Bn. Northamptonshire Regiment.   Appendix 13

The following is a list of N.C.Os. and Men awarded the MILITARY
        MEDAL, as per Divisional Routine Order No.147,d/10.9.16 :-

8239	Cpl. Stapleton	M.	"D" Coy	8277	Sgt.Sullivan	W.	"C" Coy.
13104	Sgt. Tack	E.W.	"C" "	12766	Cpl.Alleway	E.	"B" "
3/10888	Pte. Blunt	H.	"C" "	13396	Pte.Stevens	S.	"D" "
14856	" Adams	G.	"D" "	13945	" Sanders	G.H.	"B" "
13138	" Walker	W.H.	"B" "	14495	Cpl.Radley	L.	"A" "
13968	Sgt. Freeman	J.	"D" "	15592	L/C.Roberts	L.J.	"D" "
13908	Pte. Golding	G.	"C" "	13830	Pte.Shrive	C.	"A" "

Ah well, didn't get one; pity really.

17th   The battalion paraded for Divine Service at 10 a.m.

Yes, the service certainly does help to create a bit of inner peace.

~~18th~~ "   Coy training. Certain Officers, N.C.O.s & men attended a Stokes Mortar demonstration at RAINCHEVAL. C.O., 2nd – in – Command, Adjutant, Coy Commanders, & 2nd-in-Command of Coys attended a Brigade conference at RAINCHEVAL at 4 p.m.

It's been an interesting day today and to get out and about to the Stokes Mortar demonstration gave us a break. It was also interesting when, looking back and thinking about it, I didn't get the usual nervous reaction to the explosions and my stomach feels much, much better. It's either I'm getting used to the noise of war or the scoff's improving.

18th   In morning the battalion went on a route march. All Officers attended a battalion conference in afternoon.

ARQUÈVES

Sept. 19   For conspicuous gallantry & devotion to duty the following decorations were awarded :-
Capt. O.D. SHREINER – Military Cross, Capt. S le FLEMING SHERERD – Military Cross
No. 16734 ~~Sgt.~~ C.S.M. H.R PEET – D.C.M., No. 15840 Pte F.J.D. RUSSELL – D.C.M.

Those lads deserved their medals and they're bloody lucky to be alive to get them. Good on y'er lads, well done.

"   20   Coy training in morning. All companies practiced attack formation – One platoon per Coy gave demonstration in intensive digging under Bde. instructions.

I'm not a fan of this intensive digging malarkey, well, not until the need arises.

In afternoon inspection of the battalion by C.O.

"   21   In morning, Coy training – The afternoon was devoted to interior economy, 'turn-out", inspection of clothing, equipment, etc.

I wish we could turn-out these lice, they're really, really irritating.
The medal of St. George, 4th class was awarded to No. 15840 Pte F.J.D. RUSSELL.

More and more medals being awarded. Should I do something to get one? Naaaaaaaaaaaaa, just keep your head down Bob.

        2nd Lt. N.R. HUNTING joined the battalion on 19th inst. & was posted to C. Coy.

22nd Coy training in morning. The battalion practiced the attack in afternoon.

THE BATTLE OF THIEPVAL RIDGE

HEDAUVILLE

23rd   Physical training in early morning – Bn. left at 9-15 a.m. & marched to HEDAUVILLE, where it camped.

Hedauville, considering the circumstances, is quite nice, there's even a few trees left standing.

S BLUFF AUTHUILLE

25th   The battalion paraded at 7-15 a.m. & marched to S BLUFF arriving about 10-30 a.m.
C.O. & 2nd-in-Command attended a Bde. Conference at PASSERELLE DE MAGENTA at 11 a.m. & received instructions for the attack on THIEPVAL on the morrow.

See Appendix 14
Operation Order No. 38

Authuille is in a valley and on the left, there's lots of little lakes between the river constrictions – I'm trying to picture what it may have looked like before the destruction – I bet it'll be very pretty when all this is over; I hope it won't be destroyed beyond recognition.

Here we go again. I wonder where this Thiepval Ridge is. Even when we look at the map, there's never any real village names to give us some inkling of where we are. Wherever this Ridge is, we're to attack it. Better check the gear and make sure it's clean and ready to do the business.

It appears that we'll be in support so the news isn't all that bad. The ringing in my head's getting louder.

I wonder what cleaning duties I'll get before we move.

Appendix 14

SECRET   OPERATION ORDERS No.38

War Diary

By Colonel G.E.Ripley,   24.9.16

Commanding 6th (S) Bn. Northamptonshire Regiment.

Reference Map Sheet 57 D.S.E. 1/20,000

1. MOVE.
   The Battalion will move to Dug-outs in South Bluff and AUTHUILLE.

   ROUTE.
   BOUZINCOURT, W.7. Central., W.2.b.6.0., South end of MARTIN-SART WOOD, W.9.b.8.0. through C in CEMETERY (in W.16.b.) W.5.a.4.0. BLACK HORSE ROAD.

   STARTING POINT AND TIME.
   Head of Column will be at Cross roads P.24.c.8.3. at 7-15 am. in the following order :-   Headquarters, "D", "A", "B", "C", Coy Cookers, Mess Carts, Water carts, Maltese cart and Baggage Wagon.

   xxxxxxxx . INTERVAL.
   After BOUZINCOURT Coys will march to their destination at ten minutes interval.

   ADVANCED PARTY.
   2nd Lieut F.D.S.Walker, 4 C.Q.M.Ss and Sergt.Jakes will report to the Staff Captain at the West end of BLACK HORSE ROAD (W.5.a.4.0.) at 8.30 a.m.

   OFFICERS' VALISES.
   Offices' Valises will be dumped near Bn.H.Qrs before marching off.

   OFFICERS' MESS CARTS.
   Officers' Mess Carts will be packed by 6.30 a.m.

WATER.
   All Water bottles will be filled tonight.

LEWIS GUN CARTS.
   Lewis Gun Carts will travel in rear of their respective Coys

CLEANLINESS OF BILLETS.
   All Billets will be left thoroughly clean, Os.C.Coys reporting to this Adjutant that this order has been carried out.

OFFICERS' KITS.
   Officers' Kits that are required for the trenches must be ready by 6 a.m.

                (Sgd) W.Barkham, Lieut & Adjt.
                6th (S) Bn. Northamptonshire Regiment

THIEPVAL

26   Assault on and capture of THIEPVAL.   See Appendix 15

Appendix 15.

(1) Map Sheet 57D.S.E. Square R.

(2) Plan of THIEPVAL, showing approximate line held by 6th Northants rgt. 12" Middlesex Rgt. & 11th R. Fusiliers on night of Sept. 26/27.

(3) Sketch map of THIEPVAL. showing objectives.

(4) Preliminary Instructions for the attack

(5) Operation Order No. 39

(6)   "   "   No. 40

(7) Narrative of the part played by the 6th (S) Bn. Northamptonshire Rgt. in the capture of THIEPVAL, including list of those mentioned for conspicuous gallantry & summary of casualties.

Appendix 15 - Map Sheet 57ᴰ·S.E. Square R.
(extract from map on page 101 of WO-95-2044-2_1)

Plan showing approximate position ②
of 54th Bde. on night of 26/27th Sept. 1916

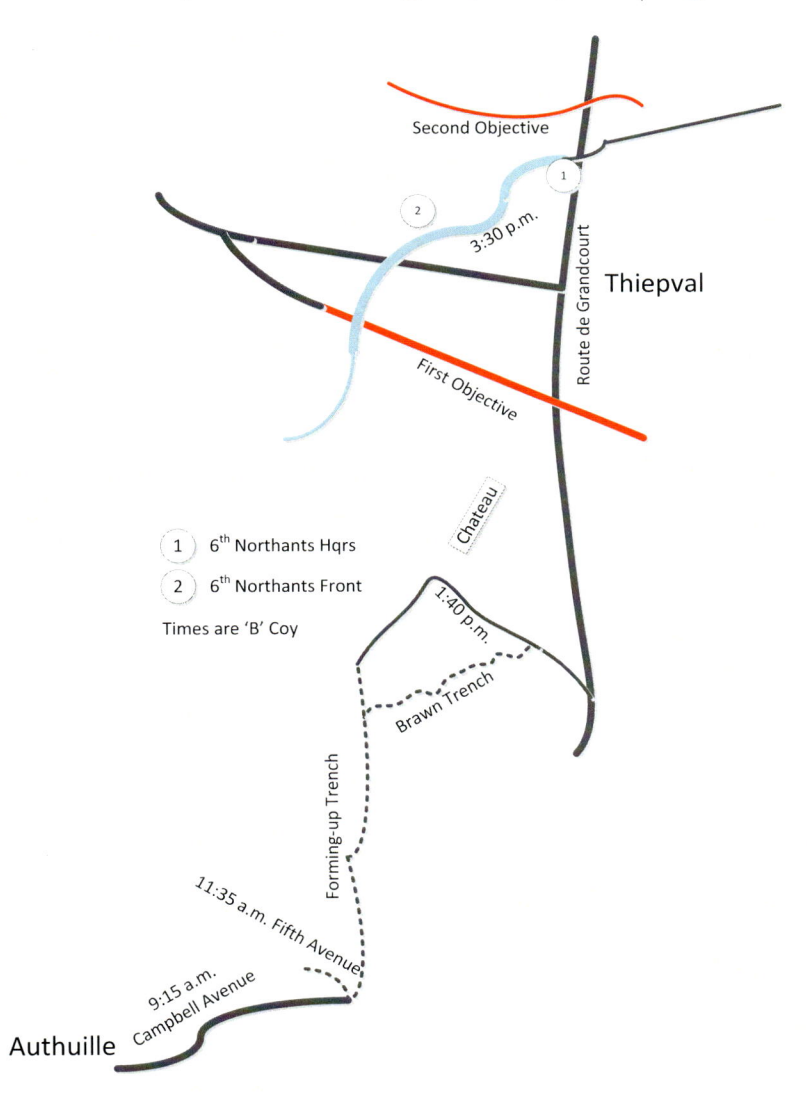

Second Objective

1 3:30 p.m.
2
Thiepval
Route de Grandcourt

First Objective

Chateau

1 6th Northants Hqrs
2 6th Northants Front
Times are 'B' Coy

1:40 p.m.
Brawn Trench

Forming-up Trench

11:35 a.m. Fifth Avenue

9:15 a.m. Campbell Avenue

Authuille

95

SECRET   6th (S) Bn. Northamptonshire Rgt.
                    ~~54TH Inf. Bde~~.

④

Preliminary Instructions for Attack.

Ref.Map Sheet. 57 d. S.E. 1/20,000   25th Sept 1916

1.   The Reserve Army is about to make a general attack on the ridge which runs from N.W. of COURCELETTE to the SCHWABEN REDOUBR.
The 18th Div. is the left Div. in the attack with the 11th Div. on its right.
The dividing line between formations is shown on the special map thus
The objectives of the 18th Div are marked on the special map:-
         First Objective.....   Blue line.
         Second   "   ......   Green Line
         Final   "   ......   Red Line.
The main line to be consolidated in read of the final objective is shown on the map thus :-
The 18th Div. will attack with the 53rd Bde on the right and the 54th Bde on the Left. The 55th Bde will be in Div.Reserve.
The 146th Inf Bde (47th Div) will continue to hold its present line.

2. TASK OF 54th INF. BDE.
     The task of the 54th Bde is to capture and hold the final objective and take every opportunity of exploiting success by pushing forward patrols and Lewis Guns to inflict casualties on retiring enemy.

3. DISTRIBUTION OF BDE AT ZERO HOUR.
     (see appendix "A" attached).

4. ROLE OF BATTALIONS.
     12th Midd'x Regt.will act as the assaulting Battn. and fight its way through to the final objective. It will first consolidate the line shownx on the special map.

5. 11th Royal Fusiliers.
     The special task of the 11th R.Fusiliers is to capture the BOSCHE front line from R.31.a.6.9 to R.25.a.9.1 and clear all

dugouts South of the trench running from R.25.b.7.3 to 25.b.3.4. To ensure that the 12th Midd'x Regt is neither attacked in flank from the Bosche front line ~~its line~~ trench named or from the rear by xxxxxxxxxxx any enemy that may come out of dug-outs after assaulting battalion has passed.

Battalion will be distributed as follows :-

One Coy detailed for special task of clearing the present BOSCHE front line trench from R.31.a.6.9. to R.25.a.9.1. at the latter point it will establish a xxxxx block.

One Coy attached to the 12th Midd'x as dug-out clearing parties. This Coy will be responsible for clearing all dug-outs south of the enemy trench running from R.25.b.7.3. to R.25.b.3.4. and will not priceed beyond the trench named.. It will be allotted definite objectives for dug-out clearing by the O.C. 12th Midd'x.

One Coy for attachment to the 12th Midd'x Regt for dug-out clearing and other special purposes during the advance from the second to the final objective. This Coy will reach the first objective in sufficient time to take part in the advance of the 12th Midd'x on its final objective.

One Coy Battn.Reserve for use in support of the remaining Coys of the Battn.

6th Northants Regt.

Will act as supports to the 12th Midd'x Regt and will be prepared to support that Battn. In its advance from the second to the final objective. It will also find two platoons for carrying from the Dump referred to in parax 9.

7th Beds.Regt.

In Bde Reserve.

5. STRONG POINTS.

Strong points will be established at the points shown on special map. Those in the final objective will be made and garrisoned by the 12th Midd'x Rgt. That in the second objective by the 11th R.Fus.

The 80th Field Coy will assist in the supervision and x construction of these strong points. Strong points will be capable of accommodating and garrisoning one platoon and will be provided with Vickers guns and Stokes Mortars as stated in paras 7 and 8

6. BARRAGES.

   Details regarding Barrages have not been received but it is understood that the form of barrage to be adopted will be a "creeping one" and it is essential that assaulting waves should follow it as closely as possible throughout the attack.

7. MACHINE GUN COY.

   Distribution of this Coy will be as follows :-
   2 guns each to the 11th R.Fus. and 12th Midd'x Rgt respectively.
   1 gun from LEIPZIG QUARRY xx xxx xxxxxxx to be detailed to proceed to Strong Point R.25.b.3.3.
   Remaining guns in LEIPZIG QUARRY in Bde Reserve.
   1 section from THIEPVAL WOOD to proceed to final objective as soon as it is consolidated. 9 guns of this section to be earmarked for strong points R.20.c.1.5. and R.19.a.5.4.
   1 section covering fire from High ground just south of HAMEL

8. 54th TRENCH MORTAR BATTERY.

   Distribution of this Battery will be as follows :-
   2 mortars each to accompany 11th R.Fus. and 12th Midd'x in the attack.
   Remainder of the Battery in Bde. Reserve.
   8 mortars to be earmarked for strong points R.30.d.1.5 and R.19x.d.4.5.

9. DUMPS.

   All Dumps will be under the control of the Bde. Bombing Officer.
   Forward dumps will be established at R.31.a.4.5. and in PAISLEY AVENUE (THIEPVAL WOOD). Carrying parties will be provided as follows :-

   For that in THIEPVAL WOOD,..   Special parties detailed from all Battns.
   For that at R.31.a.4.5.   b...   By two platoons of 6th Northants
                                                                   Regt.

10. TANKS.

    Two tanks are to be allo ted to 54th Inf.Bde. Instructions regarding their use have not been issued from Divl.H.Qrs. but all ransk should be informed that they will take part in the attack.

11. SPECIAL COMMUNICATIONS.
    As soon as the second objective is occupied a special communication trench will be constructed from our present front line trench R.25.c.5.4. to R.25.a.7.4.

12. TOOLS & S.A.A.
    Will be carried on the scale laid down for the attack on July 1st. Those required in excess of those already in possession will be drawn from LANCASHIRE DUMP.

13. MEDICAL ARRANGEMENTS.
    Will be in accordance with 18th Div.Q.M. IO of 23rd inst.

14. PRISONERS OF WAR.
    Prisoners of War will be dealt with in accordance with 18th Div.Q.R.11 f 24rd Sept. All prisoners will as far as possible be handed over to the 11th R.Fus. Where this is not possible Battalion capturing prisoners will conduct them to Divl. cage. A written receipt should be obtained for all prisoners handed in at Divl.cage. These receipts should be forwarded to Bde H.Qrs.

15. STRAGGLERS.
    Police Posts for the collection of Stragglers will be established xx under,Bde arrangements, at BLACK HORSE BRIDGE". Xxxxxxxxxxxxxxxxxxxxxxxxxxxx W end of CAMPBELL AVENUE, AUTHUILLE BRIDGE, SOUTH CASUEWAY.

16. PACK DUMPS.
    Will be selected by Battns. as follows :-
    11th R.Fus.,   in neighbourhood of QUARRY, R.31.c.3.4.
      7th Beds.   at N.BLUFF.
      6th Northants   S.BLUFF.
    12th Midd"x Regt.   under Battn.arrangements.
    Battalions will leave two men in charge of their pack Dumps.

17. RATIONS.
    Arrangements will be in accordance with 18th Div.Q.R.IO of 23rd inst except that para 2 (b) is altered as follows :-
    1st Line Transport will deliver rations at LANCASHIRE DUMP Q.35.d.3.8. by day as early as possible. Rations will

then be transferred to tramline and conveyed to AUTHUILLE whence they will be carried by hand under Battn. arrangement.

18. GRENADES.
Instructions regarding number of grenades to be carried have been issued in S.C. 692 of 24th inst.

19. COMMUNICATIONS.
Telephone. Every effort will be made to keep lines going to Battn.Hd Qrs. Through to Bde Exchanges at CAMPBELLS POST and NORTH BLUFF. These Exchanges will always be kept open.

20. VISUAL.
Battn.H.Qrs will take forward French Signalling lamps as well as ordinary visual kit.
Divl.Reading Station is at Q.23.c.3.5. – call AU - and in full view from West side of THIEPVAL RIDGE.
D.D. messages repeated three times to be sent to this station.

RUNNERS.
Runnners returning from front should come via CAMPBELLS POST or NORTH BLUFF or PAISLEY XXX DUMP stall of which places messages can be wired on to Bde.
Bde. Runner Posts will be at CAMPBELLS POST and the BLUFF.

APPENDIX "A" Distribution of 54th Bde. immediately before ZERO hour

UNIT ~~Position~~	POSITION ~~Batt H.Q~~	H. Q. (BATTN)
12th Midd'x Rgt also ½ Sect. (2 guns) 54th M.G. Coy ½ " (2 mortars) 54th T.M.B. 1 Coy 11 R. Fus. (dug-out cleaning party)	Forming up trenches included in the Rectangle R.31.b.2.5 – a.6.6 – a.4.0. – c.6.9 – d.2.6 (less the actual trench running from R.31.a.6.6 to R.31.d.H.8.	H.Q. 12th Midd'x in dug-outs immediately South of R.31.a.7.2
2 Coys 11th R. Fusiliers Also ½ Sec. (2 guns) 54th M.G. Coy ½ " (2 mortars) 54th T.M.B.	In Trench R.31.a.6.6 – d.4.8 and new communication trench from old British front line leading into old German front line N. of Point R.31.a.5.5.	
11th R. Fus. (less 2 Coys) also – 1 Sec. 54th M.G. Coy	In LEMBERG TRENCH and QUARRY	H.Q. 11th R. Fus. In dugouts at R.31.c.6.8
2 Secs. 80th F. Coy R.E.	In tunnel west of R.3.1.a.5.3	
6th Bn NORTHANTS 1 Company 1 Company 2 Coys	In old German trench between X.1.b.1.8 – 1.a.3.8 and old British front line South of that trench In CAMPBELL AVENUE In dug outs SOUTH BLUFF	H.Q. 6th Northants in CAMPBELLS POST Q.36.a.2.2
7TH BEDS ROT. 2 Companies 2 Companies	In dug-outs NORTH BLUFF In PAISLEY AV. (THIEPVAL WOOD)	H.Q. 7th Beds in NORTH BLUFF
2 Secs 80th F. Coy R.E. } 1 Sec 54th M.G. Coy	In PAISLEY AV. (THIEPVAL WOOD)	
1 Sec 54th M.G. Coy	In positions on HAMEL-MESNIL Ridge (to bring direct over-head fire during attack	
H.Qrs 54th M.G. Coy } 54th T.M.B (Less 1 Sec.)	In NORTH BLUFF	

OPERATION ORDERS No.39.
By Colonel G.E.Ripley   In the Field.
Comm nding 6th (S) Bn. Northamptonshire Regiment   25.9.16.

Ref. Maps.
ST. PIERRE DIVION   ⎫
THIEPVAL   ⎬ 1/5000
57 D. S.E.   1/20,000
& Special maps issued

1. PRELIMINARY INSTRUCTIONS.
   (1) Orders with regard to the following dispositions and objectives.

   (2) TASK OF 54th INF.BDN.
         (3) Distribution of Bde. at ZERO hour.
         (4) Role of Battalions.
         (5) Strong Points.
         (6) Barrage.
         (7) Machine Gun Coy.
         (8) 54th T.M. Battery.
         (9) Dump.
         (10) Tanks.
         (11) Special Communication.
         (12) Tools nd S.A.A.
         (13) MEDICAL ARRANGEMENTS.
         (14) Prisoners of War.
         (15) Stragglers.
         (16) Pack Dumps.
         (17) Rations.
         (18) Grenades.
         (19) Communications.
           Have already been issued in the form of Preliminary Instructions.

   CORRIGENDA.
       Para (1) for "between formations on the special map thus" read *for this* "by track running through R.31.a.b., 25.d.d., 19.b. 20.c."
       Para (1) for "Final objective is shown on Special Map thus" *for this* read "by red dotted line."

2. ZERO HOUR.
    The time for Zero Hour will be notified as soon as known.

3. DISTRIBUTION AT ZERO HOUR.
    One hour before Zero Hour "B" Coy will be formed up in CAMPBELL AVENUE, "C" Coy will be formed up in the old German front line trench which faces South in X.1.a. and will move into this trench via BURY STREET and CHOWBENT STREET., "A" Coy (with a platoon of "D" Coy attached)"will remain in dug –outs in South Bluff till receipt of further orders., xxxxxxxxxxxxxxxxxxxxxxxxxxx 2 platoons of "D" Coy will be employed at the Dump at R.31.a.5.3. under the orders of the Bde Bombing Officer. Orders will be issued later as to the time this party will report themselves to the Dump.

4. ROLE OF THE 6th BN. NORTHANTS REGT.
    The role of the 6th Bn. Northants Regt. will be that of the Supporting Battalion to 12th Bn. Midd'x Regt.
    "B" and "C" Coys must be in such a position that they can reinforce the 12th Bn. Midd'x Regt. as quickly as possible if required. Too ensure this they must keep close in rear of the fourth Coy of the 11th Bn.R.Fusiliers who will be acting in co-operation with the 12th Bn. Midd'x Regt (vide para 4 Preliminary Instructions) unless required in support of the 12th Bn. Midd'x Regt. Neither Coys will proceed North of Track running east and west , South of THIEPVAL and shown on special map in red dotted line. Either or both Coys will act in Support of the 12th Bn. Midd'x Regt in receiving a written order from O.C. 12th Bn. Midd'x Regt. and will act under orders.   "B" Coy will advance first in rear od fourth Coy R. Fusiliers, its route will be from CAMPBELL AVENUE along old German front line to "forming up" trench in R.31.a.8.6. – 7.5 – 9.4. and thence to R.35.c.5.4. to D-1.2.
    "C" Coyx will advance in rear of "B" Coy, its route will be from its "forming up" trench via CABBAGE STREET to the "forming up" trench in R.a.5.3. – 8.3. – 9.3. and thence to R.25.a.6.4. to R.31.b.5.9.
    In the event of the 12th Bn. Midd'x Regt being unable to advance to the attack on the final objective the 6th Bn. Northants may be called upon to undertake this attack. In this case a re-bombardment will be ordered and the new operation will be inaugurated xx xxx under the command of O.C. 6th Bn. Northants Rgt.

An hour for re-bombardment will be given and Zero hour will commence half an hour after the hour notified.

5. LIAISON.
   The strictest Liason must be maintained between "B" and "C" Coys and also between "D" Coy and 4th Coy 11th R.Fusiliers

6. FLARES.S.O.S. SIGNALS & COMMUNICATIONS WITH AEROPLANES.
   Instructions have been issued.

7. WATER.
   Water bottles must be full at ZERO hour and all ranks must be made to understand that the water in their bottle will have to last them till nightfall. A small supply of water only will be obtainable at CAMPBELL POST and PAISLEY AVENUE (THIEPVAL WOOD).

8. RATIONS.
   One day's rations and one day's irion rations will be carried.

9. HEADQUARTERS.
   6th Bn. Northants Regt Hd.Qrs will be at Zero hour at CAMPBELL POST and will move to R.31.a.7.8. about one hour later.
   12th Bn. Midd'x Rgt Hd.Qrs at Zero hour at R.31.a.7.8. and will move to first objective about one hour later.
   11th Bn. R.Fusilliers will be at ZERO hour at R.31.o.6.8. and will move to near first objective about one hour later.

10. INFORMATION.
    No effort must be spared to send backinformation to Bn.H.Qrs. When sending back a report of a situation not obtained by by personal observation the sources of information must always be clearly stated.

11. BARRAGE.
    Should any coy of the 6th Bn. Northants Regt be in the front line all ranks must remember to keep within 40 to 50 yards of our barrage. When the Barrage stops they stop. When it moves on again they move on also

12. MEDICAL ARRANGEMENTS.
   Stretcherbearers will remain with their Coys and will take orders from their coy Commanders.
   All Sanitary men will be in reserve and will report to the M.O. at Bn.Hd.Qrs.
   Walking wounded will make their way to Advanced Dressing Station at BLACK HORSE BRIDGE.
   As the Advance proceeds other Advanced Dressing Stations will be opened. Information concerning these will be sent to Coys as fresh stations are opened.
   When final objective is reached Regtl.Ad Post will be opened near Bn.Hd.Qrs.

13. WATCHES.
   Os.C.Coys will synchronize their watches at Battn.Hd.Qrs before leaving their present position.

14. SMALL ENTRENCHING TOOLS & DUG-OUT FRAMES.
   These will be sent up as oportunity permits by O.C. Dumps.

P
(Sgd) W.Barkham, Lieut & Adjt.
6th (S) Bn. Northamptonshire Regiment.

Copy No.	1	"A" Coy
	2	"B" "
	3	"C" "
	4	"D" "
	5.	Bde.
	6	Hd.Qrs.
	7	War Diary.

SECRET. No 1

OPERATION ORDERS No. 40 ⑥
By Colonel G.E.Ripley, In the Field
Commanding 6th (S) Bn. Northamptonshire Regiment. 26.9.16.
----

1. ZERO HOUR.

   Zero hour will be at 12.35 p.m. today, 26th inst.
   All Units are to be in position by 10.30 a.m. instead of as stated in Operation Order No. 30, para 3.

2. STRONG POINTS.

   The Strong Point in the Final Objective at R.20.d.1.5. will now be garrisoned by the 53rd Inf.Bde instead of as stated in Preliminary Instructions, para 5.

3. DUMPS.

   The forward Dumps at R.31.a.4.5 and Q.30.d.6.1. will be moved forward to R.25.c.9.4. and R.25.b.4.9. respectively as soon as circumstances permit.

4. TANKS.

   One "TANK" will emerge from the small copse at Q.30.d.3..0 at Zero hour and proceed in the direction of THIEPVAL Chateau. It should arrive at the Chateau ruins at approximately the xxxx same time as the leading infantry. This "TANK" will be followed by a second "TANK". These two tanks will remain in THIEPVAL to assist the Infantry in clearing the village. As soon as the Infantry advance on the final objective the two "TANKS" will accompany them. Their objective will be th SCHWABEN REDOUBT.

5. FLARES.

   The leading line of Infantry will light flares at the following times :-

   (a) Forty eight minutes after ZERO.
   (b) xx Two hours, fifteen minutes after ZERO.
   (c) Three hours, thirty minutes after ZERO.

   or at any time on demand being made from Contact Aeroplanes sound Klaxon horns or dropping white Verey lights.

6. DISTINGUISHING FLAG.
    The leading wave of the 12th Midd'x Rgt. will carry a large yellow and red flag in order to show the Infantry in rear and the "tanks" their position.

7. EQUIPMENT.
    In addition to normal fighting equipment the following will be carried :-
    One bandolier in addition to equipment ammunition. (170 rounds in all).
    One waterproof sheet.
    All men will wear one Smoke helmet in the "alert" position.

8. TIME IN POSITION.
    All Coys will inform Bn.H.Qrs immediately they are in position.

9. PRISONERS OF WAR.
    Reference "Preliminary Instructions, para 14 Prisoners of War". Receipts obtained on delivery of prisoners at Divl.cages should be handed to any of the Bde. Police at Stragglers Posts.

10. WATER SUPPLY.
    There will be a water supply in THIEPVAL WOOD at ROSS CASTLE XX Q.30.b.6.1. By the afternoon, there will also be a a supply of water at JOHNSTONE POST, Q.30.d.8.2. Filled petrol tins will be taken forward to Dumps.

11. CARRYING PARTIES FOR DUMPS.
    The two platoons of "D" Coy mentioned in Operation Order No.39, para 3. will report to the Bde. Bombing Officer at the Dump at R.31.a.5.3. at ~~8.30~~ a.m.
    10.30

12. PACK DUMPS.
    All packs will be dumped by 9 a.m. near East end of BLACK HORSE STREET.

13. SECRECY OF ORDERS.
    Compete copies of orders and instructions or maps of our Trenches must not be taken into action, only sufficient

notes made from them should be carried in writing as are necessary for reference.

    Os.C.Coys will **xxxxxx** return their copies of orders to Bn. H.Qrs before moving up to Front Line trenches.

                    (Sgd) W.Barkham, Lieut & Adjt.
                      6th (S) Bn. Northants Regt.

    Copies No. 1 "A" Coy
                2. "B" "
                3. "C" "
                4. "D" "
                5. Bde.
                6. Hd.Qrs.
                7. War Diary.

Got detailed to go into the attack with the 12th Middlesex. Why's it always me? Why can't I just get an easy life and stay with the lads in reserve. Ah well, perhaps I'll get lucky and get a medal without getting wounded. Love you our Trudy.

We've been told, as I'd guessed, that the tactics had been changed. They said that by attacking at dawn, it gave the Germans time to counter-attack and by leaving it till midday, they wouldn't have time to counter-attack before dark. Mmm, sounds about right to me.

We've also been told that we're to have armoured tanks with us but as they weren't a great success during their first use a few days ago on the 15th, I'm not confident but let's see shall we Bob.

Narrative of the part played by the 6th S. Bn.
Northamptonshire Regiment in the capture of
THIEPVAL on the 26th September 1916.

Copies of preliminary instructions, Operation Orders
and Sketch Maps are attached.

Here we go; more blood and guts. Follow the leader and keep your bloody head down Bob. Quite a nice morning though but quite nippy; the breeze's not helping. Looks as though it'll warm up when the sun breaks through but we've been told that there's a slight chance of a bit of rain.

Remember Bob, it's not your time to take a bullet; just concentrate and the rest will look after itself. I can feel my heart beating faster, my bubble closing in, my senses changing, relaxing, focusing...

At 9-15 a.m. "B" Company left their dug-outs in SOUTH BLUFF
to move into their "Forming up" Trench in CAMPBELL AVENUE.
"C" Company followed a few minutes later, and proceeded
to their "Forming-up" Trench in R.31.c.6.0. to X.1.A.6.8.
At 9-30 a.m. Battalion Headquarters left South BLUFF and
proceeded to their First Battle Headquarters at CAMPBELL POST
arriving there at 10 a.m., **xxxxx**
At 10 a.m. two platoons "D" Company left SOUTH BLUFF under
2nd Lieuts HIGHAM and SCOTT-*TAGGART* and reported themselves
to Officer Commanding Dump at CAMPBELL POST as Carrying parties.
At 10-19 a.m. and 10-30 a.m. "B" and "C" Companies had respectively taken up their positions in their "Forming-up" Trenches.
At 11.23 a.m. 2.Lt Goddard "B" Company, reported thathe was in
touch with the rear Company of 11th Royal Fusiliers, who were

then moving up from LEMBERG TRENCH via PRINCE STREET.
At 11-35 a.m. "B" Company arrived at FIFTH AVENUE.
At 1 p.m. "C" Company left their "Forming-up" Trench and began to move forward. By this time an extremely heavy Enemy Barrage was being put on all communication Trenches leading up to the Front Line and Battalion Headquarters at CAMPBELL POST was being shelled by heavy H.E. shells – one shell bust in trench three yards from Headquarter Dug-out, blowing to pieces the three men in next dug-out.

Stay behind the tank. They said take the BRAWN trench to the right for more cover. Crack, crack, thud - he crumples, crack, ting, ting, metal on metal, crack, crack, ting, thud - nobody falls. Protect the bubble, keep going crack… crack… crack.

At 1-23 p.m. a message was received from "C" Company stating that Captain Evans, and 2 Lt Bailey had become casualties.
At 1-40 p.m. "B" Company arrived in Trench just SOUTH of the CHATEAU, though news of their arrival there was not received until 3-30 p.m. At this time Battalion Headquarters – although no news had been received from 12th Middlesex Regt. that their Headquarters at R.31.c.66. had been vacated – decided to transfer their Headquarters there. Owing to the extremely heavy Barrage, a considerable amount of disorganization took place during the move, and many units of Headquarters became cut off by the Barrage, or owing to the trenches being obliterated by shell fire, lost their direction.
On arrival at INVERARY TRENCH just East of R.31.A.4.2. one H.E. shell wounded Colonel Ripley badly in the arm and Lieut and Adjutant Barkham in the leg and arm. The former was put into a dug-out and shortly afterwards attended to by the Medical Officer.
Just before leaving CAMPBELL POST, under instructions received from Brigade Headquarters, "A" Company and "D" Company (less two platoons) had been sent orders by 2 Lieut Frend to proceed

immediately to the Road SOUTH of the CHATEAU, and reinforce the 12th Middlesex.

At 2-45 p.m. I proceeded with 2 Lieut Walker and four runners, the only Headquarters personnel which could be collected, to take up my Headquarters in R.31.c.6.6., and take over command of the Battalion.

At 2-30 p.m. "A" Company and "D" Company (less two platoons) had left SOUTH BLUFF and commenced their advance to the Road SOUTH of the CHATEAU.

On arrival at R.31.c.6.6. I found that dug-out lately occupied by the 12th Middlesex Headquarters was choked with wounded. A Brigade Report Centre was established there, but all Telephone wires had been cut and the only possible communication was by runners or pigeons.

At 3-30 p.m. my Signalling Officer, 2 Lt Margoliouth arrived with about six Signallers.

It was about this time that "C" Company arrived in trench just SOUTH of the CHATEAU.

2nd Lt. Hayward being the only Officer left with the Company, this Officer very shortly afterwards became a casualty, and as the Sergeant Major had also been put out of action earlier, the command of the Company devolved on Sergeant Pullen who carried out his duties with the greatest courage and coolness. This Company under orders from O.C. 12th Middlesex Regiment were sent to reinforce the 11th Royal Fusiliers who were held up on the left of the line N.W. of the CHATEAU. During the ensuing night they were used to hold a portion of the line on the flank.

"B" Company in the meantime had moved forward to support the 12th Middlesex Regt., in the centre of the line near Second Objective.

Immediately on leaving the CHATEAU, Machine gun fire and

fire from Snipers hidden in the shell holes was very deadly especially on the Left Flank.

It was whilst advancing from the CHATEAU that Capt Batty gallantly leading his men. was severely wounded. and 2nd Lt Stone killed. 2nd Lieuts Goddard and Nendick having been previously wounded, this Company was in a similar plight to "C" Company, and was without any Officers. The Acting-Sergt Major, Sergt Partridge, then assumed command of the Company and carried on with the greatest gallantry.

At 4 p.m., half an hour after "B" and "C" Companies had gone forward from the CHATEAU, "A" Company and two platoons of "D" Company arrived on the scene and immediately advanced to the support of the Front Line on the centre and right of the second Objective.

Captain Stokes, commanding "A" Company was wounded before arriving at the CHATEAU, 2nd Lieut Keys was wounded by rifle-fire whilst leading the Company across the open to the North of the CHATEAU and 2nd Lieut Frend had also been put out of action. The situation with regard the Officers of the 6th S. Bn. Northamptonshire Regiment in the Front Line was therefore as follows :-

    "B" Company – No Officers, Sgt Partridge in Command
    "C"   "   - "   "   Sgt Pullen in Command
    "A"   "   - One Officer. 2nd Lieut Gotch in Command
    "D" Company (less 2 platoons) 2nd Lieut Bates in Command.

At 4-30 p.m. Lieut Ashmole 11th Royal Fusiliers, 54th Infantry Brigade Liason Officer arrived at my Headquarters and I gave him the situation as far as I had learnt it, from two messages for Brigade Headquarters just received from Lieut Col Maxwell, from the CHATEAU, and which had been forwarded one by runner and one by pigeon.

As I had now been informed that my last two remaining Companies

had arrived at the CHATEAU, I decided to move my Headquarters there, leaving 2nd Lieut Margoliouth and his Signallers at the Report Centre to try and obtain communication.
Accompanied by 2nd Lieut Walker and four Runners only, as I did not know if there would be accomodation for my Headquarters Staff, as well as that of the 12th Middlesex Regiment, at the CHATEAU. I arrived there about 5-15 p.m. – Here I found Lieut-Col. Maxwell and his Headquarters Staff.
After being informed of the situation in front as far as it was known, Lieut-Col. Maxwell directed me to proceed to the Front Line to clear up the situati n, and take command of the Front Line on the Right and Centre. A considerable amount of Sniping and Machine Gun Fire was still coming from the enemy on out left flank. which continued until night-fall.
After getting into touch with Lieut Odgers 12th Middlesex Rgt, and 2nd Lt. Bates and Gotch of my Battalion, I managed to visit most of that part of the line before dusk and found *it* to run as shown on accompanying sketch.

6th. Northamptonshire Regiment and 12th Middlesex Regiment were somewhat mixed up, whilst a few Royal Fusiliers were on the Right of the Line which was in touch with the 10th Essex.
Owing to the lateness of the hour and the near approach of dusk, I decided that it was not feasable to straighten out the line, but preferable to consolidate the lin already held.
I accordingly sorted out Battalions as well as possible, filled up all gaps, withdrew a few small isolated detachments that were too far advanced and liable to be cut off or come under our own fire and commenced to consolidate the line.
Several Bombing Posts and Blocks were also established in Communication Trenches, which led towards the enemy.
Lieut Odgers with two Subalterns was in command of the Right

of the Line, and I placed 2nd Lt Gotch in Command of the Right half Battalion 6th Northants, and 2nd Lieut Bates in Command of Left half of the Battalion, in the Centre of the Line. The latter informed me that he was in touch with the 11th Royal Fusiliers on his left and so, as I knew there was a Captain of the 11th Royal Fusiliers on that part of the Line, I did not visit it.

It was not until about 11-30 p.m. that I was able to send Lieut Col Maxwell a Report of the situation, at which time I had managed to establish my Headquarters in a dug-out in the front Line near R.25.B.4.2.

Except for a certain amount of promiscuous shelling between our Line and the CHATEAU" **XXXXXXXXXXXXXXXXXX** the night passed fairly quietly. At 5-30 *a*.m. two companies of the 7th Bedfords passed through our lines to take the German Front Line on our left flank.

At the same time the personnel of an Enemy Dressing Station consisting of one Officer and about twenty other ranks came over to us and gave themselves up as prisoners. They were all spotlessly clean and it did not appear as though they had been attending to the duties of their profession.

At 8 a.m. "A" Company 7th Bedfords arrived, and I informed Lieut Odgers that he could withdraw his Battalion. As soon as he was clear I withdrew my Battalion, except "C" Company, who were on the left of the line and were withdrawn under orders direct by Lieut Col. Maxwell.

The withdrawal was carried out with practically no casualties in spite of a certain amount of hostile shelling.

I wish to bring to notice the names of the following Officers N.C.O-s and Men for special acts of gallantry or devotion to duty during the above operation.

       2nd Lt. F.D.S. Walker
       Capt E.A. Bennet   C. to F.
       2.Lt.   A.C.Bates
       2.Lt   D.I.Gotch
       Lieut C.G.Kemp   R.A.M.C.

No. 13475 Sgt. (Acting C.S.M.) Partridge J.W.
     13537 "   F.C.Pullen
     17416 "   W.L.Miles
     7985   "   F. Rowlands
     14584 "   W.T.Scriven
     14036 Pte W.G.Coe
     10914 L/Cpl A.F.Simmons
     14310 Sgt. A.G.Bury
     15087 L.Cpl T. Thompson
     14309 Pte. G. Byrne
     32279 Pte A.Tebbett
     13451 L.Cpl F. Shipton
     22119 Pte J. Walsh
     14631 L. Cpl F. Hill
     15386 Cpl. Scott. W.A.

                           Major
           Commdg 6th S. Bn. Northamptonshire Regt.

Subject. Operations.

From.   Officer Commanding
                6th. S. Bn. Northampton hire Regt.

To.   Headquarters,
            54th Brigade

Reference my N.R.A. 606 of yesterday, I should like to add the following names to those appearing on page 4 of my Narrative.-

2 Lt Keys C.G.
NXXX No. 43082 Pte Grace H.C.
    No. 15910 " Mayes. S.

Appendix F. is also forwarded to be attached.

                                Major
Commdg. 6th. S.Bn.Northamptonshire Regt.

In the Field
2.10.16

6th (S) Bn Northamptonshire Regiment.

SUMMARY OF CASUALTIES.

2nd Lt STONE,	WILLIAM HENRY.	KILLED in ACTION		26.9.16
" " HAYWARD,	HERBERT WILLIAM.	"	"	"
CAPTAIN EVANS,	DOUGLAS LANE.	Died of wounds		27.9.16
" BATTY	GEOFFREY GEORGE HORN	"		"
COLONEL RIPLEY.	GEORGE EUSTACE.	Wounded in Action		26.9.16
Lt. & Adj BARKHAM.	WILLIAM HENRY.	"	"	"
CAPTAIN STOKES.	EVAN FRASER.	"	"	"
2nd Lt. GODDARD	HAROLD WILLIAM.	"	"	"
" NENDICK,	LAURENCE.	"	"	"
" KEYS,	CLEMENT GEOFFREY.	"	"	"
" FREND.	HUGH PALLISER.	"	"	"
" SMYTH,	NUGENT.	"	"	"
" BAILEY,	LESLIE CHARLES.	"	"	"

The following are other Ranks.

    Killed...24
    Wounded...105
    Missing..17
    Suffering from Shell Shock..................5
    Wounded and Missing..........................3
    Missing believed Killed..... 2

                                    Major
                    Commdg. 6th (S) Bn Northamptonshire Regiment.

In the Field.
2 / 10 / 16.

I'm tired. What the hell happened? Slaughter everywhere. Shit, guts and mud everywhere. Bloody explosions, cracks, thuds and more explosions, but I don't think I got hit. I think I'm OK, I don't feel any pain. Christ, my head's ringing like a church bell. Christ, how did I manage that? God knows who's left. Christ, I just feel sooooo tired.

Thank Christ for that, we're being relieved. I'm not sure how much more of this I can take.

S BLUFF

Sept 27 The battalion having been relieved in THIEPVAL by the 7th Bedfords, ~~retn~~ at 8 a.m. returned to dug-outs at S. BLUFF by about 10 a.m.

It appears that we captured Thiepval and from what is being bandied about, it's a great victory. But at what cost – shit, it was unreal. Comrades blasted to pieces or left in agony until the body snatchers could rescue them. Men wandering around with shell shock not knowing what they're doing. Brave young men, with families and bright futures, mowed down, killed or maimed for life. For what; a piece of featureless land full of trenches, rubble, twisted metal, body parts and dead tree stumps. Another son of the village, Malcolm Magee, who I talked to before the attack, didn't make it and it's a bloody wonder I did.

28   Re-organisation of companies was commenced. Officers were placed in temporary command of companies as follows :- A Coy. 2nd Lt. D.M. HERIZ-SMITH, B Coy. 2nd Lt. C.K. CHATHAM, C Coy. 2nd Lt. F.D.S. WALKER, D Coy. 2nd Lt. WEBB.

MAILLY MAILLET WOOD

29   Inspection of arms, equipment, ammunition, etc.
The battalion left S. BLUFF about 9 p.m. and marched to MAILLY MAILLET WOOD arriving about 10-30 p.m. where the whole battalion were most hospitably entertained by the 12th Middlesex, before turning in.

I have to make myself believe it was a glorious victory because thoughts of death and destruction are so quickly forgotten over a couple of beers, backslapping and laughter. This is unreal; I did nothing more than was expected; protected my bubble while I destroyed others. I'm confused.

In a matter of hours our dead comrades are pushed to the back of our minds and here we are, celebrating; what's happening to us.

30   The battalion was inspected and congratulated by the C.O. on the glorious part it had played in the capture of THIEPVAL, the strongest enemy fortress on the whole of the Western Front. Numerous congratulatory telegrams were received.   *Appendix 16*

So, from the number of congratulatory messages being read out, it was a glorious victory and what they said was true. We took the strongest enemy fortress on the whole Western Front. The relatives back home must be told of the rewards taken for the ultimate sacrifice given by their kin; they must be told!

<u>S.H. Charrington</u> Maj.
Commdg. 6th (S) Bn.
Northamptonshire Rgt.
5/10/16

Appendix 16

18th. DIVISION.

Copies of Congratulatory Messages received by the Division on the successful operations resulting in the Capture of THIEPVAL on September 26th 1916 and of SCHWABEN REDOUBT on September 28th. 1916.

----

(1) Telegrams from Lieutenant General C.W.JACOB, C.B. Commanding 11nd. Army Corps.

"TO:- 18th. Division.
G.1881. 26th.
Corps Commander wishes to thank you and all Ranks of your Division for their admirable work today AAA THIEPVAL has withstood all attacks upon it for exactly two years and it is a great honour to your Division to have captures the whole of this strongly fortified village at their first attempt AAA Hearty congratulations to you all.

FROM:- 11nd. Corps.
9.10 p.m.

"TO:- 18th. Division.
G.1998. 28th.
     Commander
The Corps again thanks and congratulates all ranks of 18th. Division on further gallant and successful work today.AAA He specially commands

the good organisation, training and Staff Work displayed and the methodical and determined manner in which all orders and plans have been carried out and all prearranged objectives reached and consolidated.

From:- 11nd. Corps.
11/12 p.m.

(2)   Telegram from General Sir. H. de la P. GOUGH, K.C.B. Commanding Reserve Army.

"TO:- Maj.Gen.MAXSE   28.9.16.
18th. Division.

Congratulate you very heartily on success of to-days attack as well as of previous operations AAA Reflects greatest credit on you and your troops.

FROM:- General Gough.

(3)   Telegram from General Sir.HERBERT C.O.PLUMER G.C.M.G.,K.C.B. Commanding Second Army.

"TO:- Eighteenth DIVISION.
G.930.   28th.

Many congratulations to you and your Division from Commander and Staff Second Army.

FROM:- Second Army.
5-45 p.m. "

(4)   Personal congratulations of GENERAL SIR.DOUGLAS HAIG, G.C.B., G.C.V.O., K.C.I.E. Commander-in-Chief British Armies in France.

"TO:- 53rd, 54th, and 55th Infantry Brigades.
G.221.   Sept. 27th.

The Commander-in-Chief personally called to-day on General MAXSE to congratulate the Division on its success at THIEPVAL.

        From:- 18th. Division.
            4-30 p.m.

E.V.RIDDELL. Lt. Colonel,
A.A. & Q.M.G.,   18th. Division.
29th. September 1916.

THE BATTLE OF THE ANCRE HEIGHTS

MAILLY-MAILLET

1916   Return to winter time.

OCT.   At church parade which was held in conjunction with the 11th Royal Fusiliers

1   Brigadier-General SHOUBRIDGE congratulated the Brigade on the work at THIEPVAL.

All companies attended baths at HEDAUVILLE

It's getting colder by the day and they decide it's time for a bath; bloody typical. The dirt's keeping me warm but I suppose the hot water and being clean will make me feel a bit better.

A draft of 100 men joined the Battalion at night

2   Company training

Heard that Raymond Percival died yesterday; how many more men from the village will this bloody war take?

3   The Battalion entrained (H.Q two companies and the new draft at BELLE ÉGLISE two companies at ACHEUX-en-Amiénois) and proceeded to CANDAS, whence they marched to BERNEUIL, arriving at 9 p.m.

BERNEUIL

Training, training, training! When do we get a weekend off? I miss my Trudy so, so much.

4   Company training from 10 a.m. to 12 noon and from 2 p.m. to 4 p.m.

5   Company training as above

6   Company training 7-7.30 a.m. 9 a.m. to 12.30 p.m. 2 p.m. to 4 p.m.
2Lt SCOTT-TAGGART & three other ranks proceeded to a Lewis Gun Course at LE TOUQUET   2Lt WALKER proceeded on leave to ENGLAND

7   Major H.PODMORE D.S.O. rejoined Battalion · was appointed acting 2nd in-command

8   Church parade at 11 a.m. Corps Commanders proposed inspection in the afternoon was cancelled owing to inclement weather.
2Lt BOULTON & 2Lt BATHURST joined the Battalion

	9	Company training & CO's inspection in the morning. 3 hour route march in the afternoon.
	10	Lt PRICE rejoined the Battalion. 2Lt CHICK joined the battalion A draft of 17 other ranks arrived (15 being former members of the Battalion)
	11	Company Training · Major General MAXSE visited Headquarters. Lt Col CHARRINGTON went on leave
	12	Company Training in the morning : ^{inter} Company football matches in the afternoon
	13	Lt PRICE was appointed acting Adjutant.
	14	Preparations for move ~~battali~~

BEAUVAL

| | 15 | Battalion moved with rest of the 54th Bde (but independently) to BEAUVAL & billeted |

WARLOY BAILLON

| | 16 | Brigade moved into billets in CONTAY area. The Battalion in tents at WARLOY |

BOUZINCOURT

It's like I'm part of a game of chess; one minute I'm here and the next minute I'm moved somewhere else. I suppose there's method in all this movement and I suppose it keeps us occupied.

Looks like my ears are shot – they're definitely ringing all the time now. There was in intermittent period of silence and ringing but it hasn't stopped for a few days now. My guts seem to have settled a bit; although there's a constant faint pain in the middle of my belly. It really only starts to hurt a day or so before we move to the front line.

	17	Brigade moved into billets in BOUZINCOURT Battalion practiced attack in the afternoon
	18	Battalion practiced attack. C.O. Adjutant · Coy Commanders went up to reconnoitre new line in front of COURCELETTE
	19	Brigade moved into billets in ALBERT.
	20	Battalion practiced the attack

21   Lt Col CHARRINGTON returned from leave.   Battalion practiced the attack

ALBERT

22   C.O. Adjt & several officers & N.C.O.s carried out a frontier reconnaissance of forming up trenches near COURCELETTE.

23   Company parades in the morning and conference of officers & Platoon Commanders in the afternoon. Battalion attack-practice.

Grapevine says we're about to move back to the trenches. The rest was nice but I'm not looking forward to going back. Must write a letter home.

24   Preparations for move into trenches

Well, they're right, we're off to the front again. Why can't the lads get it wrong sometimes? Must finish my letter.

25   Battalion relieved 7th Bedfordshire Regiment in trenches N of COURCELETTE

I'm told the area's called the Ancre Valley after the river that runs through it and we're on the high ground looking North into the valley. Although it's not a pretty sight, you can see for miles when you get a chance to look through the periscope.

TRENCHES

    A and C Coys in REGINA TRENCH, D in Support and in VANCOUVER and HESSIAN TRENCHES, B Coy in Reserve in ZOLLERN TRENCH, H.Q. at R 29 central near Brigade H.Q.
    6 casualties in the night

More casualties during the night, poor buggers. I wonder how many shells have been fired since I came here. The amount being thrown by both sides doesn't seem to end. Where are they getting it all from? I long for the quiet, steady rhythm of Irchester.

26   Weather fairly fine. Lot continuous shelling of REGINA and VANCOUVER trenches specially on the left of REGINA which was constantly being blown in by enfilade of 5.9 guns from direction of LOUPART WOOD. About 1 a.m. two Germans came up to our parapet and gave themselves up.

	A Coys H.Q. in REGINA TRENCH was twice blown in in the early morning – Causalities 8
27	D Company relieved A Company in the left sector of REGINA trench. Keeping only two platoons in front line of REGINA trench which was in very poor condition – Casualties 14

It's Eric's birthday today – he would have been 6, poor soul. My sorrowful thoughts are also with my loving Trudy; she took Eric's death really badly and his anniversary is like a twist of the knife which's still embedded in her heart. Leonard George was killed yesterday. When will this relentless shelling stop?!

28	Continued shelling of our front and support lines by enfilade fire from the direction of LOUPART WOOD. Casualties 9

ALBERT

29	Battalion was relieved in the morning by the 8th Suffolk Regiment Day was wet and misty & so even with the bad state of trenches relief was possible over the top by day light. Last platoons returned ALBERT about 5 p.m.
	The enemy showed no activity in front but the continuous enfilade shelling of trenches which contained four traverses and no dug-outs made this a very trying tour in the trenches. Total casualties ~~50~~ 52, including 7 missing – the garrison of a ~~stron~~ standing post walk out in front of our line. Posted in the dark on the first day they must have lost their way in the next night and entered the German lines.

Funny how you get used to the continuous shelling and ever increasing number of casualties. I could never have thought, in my wildest dreams, that, in my little hole in the side of the trench, my little bubble would allow me to sleep through this din.

When I wake and over a brew, my mind easily drifts towards Irchester. My bubble, with its invisible curtain of restricted distance, sound and feel, expands to take in more of the dream but as somebody brushes past me, the bubble collapses and I'm jolted back to the grim reality I'm in.

I can see, from their very posture, many lads are in their own bubbles which are inside a bigger world bubble and through forced real world interaction the bubbles break but form again to keep everybody contained in their own perception of a safe world.

      6 officers joined the battalion on arrival in billets
      Lt J.D UNWIN to take over command of D   and   2Lieuts COWPER
      "   McWHA   A   WINKWORTH
      "   GADSDEN   B   WELFORD

30   C.O. presented two MILITARY MEDAL ribbons to the N.C.O s & men still with the battalion to whom the decoration had been awarded for gallantry at THIEPVAL. There were 19 awards in all.
The Battalion had baths.

Relaxing with my legs on the sides of a tub of hot-ish water and reading my letter from Trudy makes me feel so good. So, everything is fine at home and the children are doing well at school; lovely.

I love Irchester in autumn. The brown falling leaves, the clean crisp air, senses attuned to, "it's that time of year" and as we walk across the stubbled fields, the thoughts of the need to prepare for winter. This place would probably look and feel like home if it wasn't for the devastation but even in this hell, I, like now, occasionally get those, "it's that time of year" feeling.

WARLOY
31   Battalion moved in the morning to billets at WARLOY.

                                               S.H.Charrington Lt. Col
                                        Commdg. 6th Northamptonshire Rgt.

Nov 1916
WARLOY

1. Morning cleaning up and company drill. Afternoon inspection by the C.O.
2. Battalion paraded in the afternoon with 12th MIDDLESEX REGT and 2 battalions of 55th Bde. Major General MAXSE presented to officers & men decorations awarded since July 1 and congratulated the parade on the work done by the 18th Division since that date.

Still no medal but then again, I'm still in one piece which is more than can be said for thousands of others.

3. Battalion practiced the attack as front battalion and as third battalion in the vicinity of WARLOY & HENENCOURT.

ALBERT

4. Battalion moved to billets in ALBERT

Backwards and forwards, backwards and forwards. Can't they make up their bloody minds? In the trench, out the trench, in the trench, out the trench; Jesus Christ, make up your minds! By the time we've got ourselves clean, it's time to get dirty again.

5. Preparations for move into trenches for offensive operations

Bonfire Night, I wonder what Guy Fawkes would have made of all this? At least we don't have to go out and buy fireworks, we get them free. Thinking of the fun and laughter the kids, Trudy and me had with Bonfire Night, roasting the spuds in the fire and breaking off the burnt bits and going ooooo, aaaaaah as the rockets exploded; it got through to me a bit yesterday and I'm still feeling a bit down now.

Getting quite nippy now but at least its good underfoot and getting around's easier. It's nice of the Army to give us another chance of winning a medal. I think I'll pass them up on the honour and just look forward to getting myself back in one piece so that I can have more Bonfire Nights with the kids.

TRENCHES

6. Battalion relieved 7th Bedfordshire Regt. in same sector as before. Trenches in fair condition except VANCOUVER & much less shelling than before. Casualties 2

   B and C companies in front line

7. A very wet day reducing trenches to mud and water : no communications possible with front line except at night   Casualties 3

Jesus Christ! As soon as you get comfortable the bloody heavens open; what a bloody mess! Not only do we get shelled and shot at every hour of the day but the bloody weather adds to the misery! My feet are cold and wet and they're beginning to bloody hurt!

8. A wet day & night but very little hostile shelling. Such shelling as there was was from field guns in front and not the previous heavy gun enfilade fire. Casualty 1

I suppose the rain does have its advantages in that it reduces the shelling. My feet don't feel good.

9. A finer day : at 9.30 p.m. enemy opened heavy fire with gas and tear shells, chiefly on MOUQUET ROAD (Bn H.Q.) and ZOLLERN TRENCH.

   Gas! Shit! For Christ's sake, where's the rain when you need it?!
   This lasted with intervals till 2 a.m. there was a light wind blowing back towards the enemy and the gas reached out front line, over 1000 yds. in front, but not in quantities necessitating putting on smoke helmets. No casualties from the gas.   Casualties 4

10. A fine day. About 10 a.m. an explosion (presumably started by a bomb) occurred among bombs left by another regiment in a shelter connecting two small dug-outs. 2 men were killed and 5 wounded – all H.Q. personnel. Casualties 18

Christ, now we're being killed by our own bombs. On a good note, we can rejoice knowing that we're being relieved. Perhaps we can now get our feet dry because I have no idea what state they're in. Christ, they hurt really bad.

OVILLERS HUTS

The Battⁿ. was relieved by the 8th Suffolk Regiment and proceeded to new huts in MASH VALLEY near OVILLERS-la-Boisselle. The last man got in about 2 a.m.

WARLOY

11 The Battⁿ. moved via AVELUY and BOUZINCOURT to WARLOY. Feet were in a very bad condition but the Battⁿ. arrived at WARLOY with very few casualties (12) – a very creditable performance after the incessant wet in the trenches, where movement to keep circulation was impossible in the daytime.

12 Cleaning and refitting. Brig Gen SHOUBRIDGE personally brought the news of an immediate return to ALBERT – the Coy - expected attack being fixed at last: beginning N of the ANCRE on following day.

THE BATTLE OF THE ANCRE

ALBERT

Nov 13   Bn. moved to ALBERT via HENENCOURT – MILLENCOURT : in billets ready to move at ½ hours notice

Got my boots dried and my feet are feeling better - just in time to go back – this is not funny.

OVILLERS HUTS

14   Bn. moved to OVILLERS HUTS in the afternoon : where were 12th MIDDLESEX Rgt. and 2 Battalions of 55th Brigade

Arthur Sears was killed yesterday, poor bugger. I'm not feeling comfortable about it either because I'm not feeling the loss like I used to. I've even stopped wondering about how they died and how much of the body, if anything, they found. I'm not feeling good about my feelings but I can't seem to muster up anything but plain, unemotional thoughts these days.

15.   54th Bde. front in attack was joined to CANADIANS. 6th NORTHAMPTONSHIRE and 12th MIDDLESEX were attached to 55th Brigade.

Fine cold weather : Bn occupied in making paths & sandbagging huts.

Bit chilly but at least it's dry and the work's keeping us warm. I wonder what Trudy and the kids are doing.

16.   Fine and cold. Ground very hard & dry. General MAXSE held an officers conference explaining the operations N of ANCRE & the part of the 18th Division.

17.   Morning Coy commanders reconnoitred ways up to 55th Bde front. 1.30 a.m. orders received that Bn was to go up in support of 55th Bde. which had four battalions attacking & no reserve.

Back to the trenches again and apparently we're going to try and capture ground to the North-East.

TRENCHES

18.   Early morning Bn. moved up 3 companies to FABECK TRENCH, one company (D) to GRAVEL PIT near MOUQUET FARM (55th Bde HQ) ZERO at 6.10.

This is routine now; cracks, thuds, explosions, ducking and diving, head ringing like the proverbial church bell, the mounting list of casualties and, this is while we're still in the trench doing day-to-day routines.

My head's still on my shoulders so I must be doing something right and I don't think I'll receive any medals this time. Not nice weather; I definitely prefer snow to rain.

55th Bde attack successful – but owing to snipers left behind communication difficult and A and C Coys 6th Nth were not able to carry out the consolidation allotted to them. They arrived in FABECK for the night of the 18th with advanced H.Q. but received orders not to go forward today.

Hurray, we're over the worst and my feet are still feeling quite good. Nice to hear that we're on our way to the back lines for a rest in North West France; the down side is that we have to walk. Ah well, at least we won't get shot at and we won't have to duck and dive.

Hmmm, been in the Army for a year now. Just think, a year ago I was with all the family having my farewell dinner – Christ, I don't feel right; my eyes are watering.

It was, is, another world. A world of innocent laughter, games of chase and tag and hide and seek. Long walks to Farndish and down Green Lane and along the Sluice. What I wouldn't give for a quiet pale ale in the Red Lion now and a slice of fresh bread and dripping topped off with a dash of salt.

Christ, it's been a year; it seems like forever and yet, only yesterday. Go and have a brew with the lads Bob and bring yourself back to the reality of your life and not the real one Trudy and the kids have.

H.Q. with D and B Coys (less 50 men employed on Tramways) returned to OVILLERS HUTS.

Weather very bad : Snow began early in the morning and turned to heavy rain at night : ground became very bad indeed.

OVILLERS HUTS

19   About 6 p.m. D Coy arrived to relieve A and C Coys in FABECK TRENCH. A and C returned to OVILLERS HUTS, where the whole of the 54th Bde now was.

20   Preparations for move back to billets : one company & 50 men still in the line.

21   54th Bde began march to back area. 6th NORTHAMPTONSHIRE started from OVILLERS HUTS in the afternoon and went into tents at WARLOY.

WARLOY

     D Company relieved in time to join the Bn : the 50 men on tramways arrived a few hours later.

HERISSART

22   Continued march to back area WARLOY to HERISSART fine weather and good marching

DOULLENS

23   Continued march to DOULLENS – a long way but a fine day. Battalion marched excellently & came into billets very well –

BERNEUIL

24   Continued march to BERNEUIL – weather breaking – occasional showers

DOMQUEUR & LE PLOUY

25   Continued march to DOMQUEUR and LE PLOUY – a short march but in constant rain : billets good but very scattered

Two more days on the road and apart from the rain, spirits are quite high. Apparently we only have a bit further to go and then we can rest the feet for a while.

ONEUX

26   Continued march to ONEUX – another short stage – weather improved. In the afternoon Officers went over to see permanent billets at NEUF MOULIN

NEUF MOULIN

27   Final stage of march to NEUF MOULIN – 3 companies in the village – mostly poor billets – 1 Coy & H.Q. at the Chateau in BOIS de L'ABBAYE nearly a mile away : v.g. billets.

At last, end of the road but the billets leave a lot to be desired. Ah well, I'm sure we can make them comfortable and homely. Apparently we're about 10 miles from the coast; wonder if we'll get a chance to see the sea? Suppose not but every day now is a matter of living in hope. I wonder if there'll be a chance of a bath to soak the feet? I wonder if there's a letter from Trudy and may I even dare to think of a Red Cross parcel?

28   Refitting and drill near billets

29   Lt Col CHARRINGTON went on leave. Battalion on F area – company training

Thinking of you mum; 26 years today since you were taken from us and I still miss you deeply. I remember you making your lace at home in Astcote and the smell and warmth of long summer days in the fields. They were carefree days that I need to go back to; rest in peace mum.

30   Battalion on F area. Company training – bayonet fighting, close order drill and improving rifle range.

The boss has gone on leave, lucky bugger. When will we go; when will this war end? When can I go back to Irchester, Trudy and the kids? I know I shouldn't feel down but I've been away for so long and there seems to be no end in sight.

Come on Bob, buck up, make yourself busy, go and chat with the lads.

H. Podmore Major
Cdm 6th Northamptonshire Rgt

NEUF MOULIN

Dec 1	Company training on Areas
2	Battalion digging trenches for Brigade Attack Scheme
	Lt MARGOLIOUTH temporarily attached to 54th Bde
3	Church parades in the Chateau grounds
4	Battalion digging trenches for Brigade Attach Scheme
5	Battalion practiced role of 3rd Battn in Bde Attack
6	Capt. V.P. MOBBS joined the battalion
6	Battalion practiced first battalion in attack.
7	Company training on areas

Same old stuff, day after day but at least it's nice and quiet and nobody's shooting at us.

8	Battalion practiced 4th battalion in attack.
9	Bde practiced attack. 6th Northamptonshire 4th Battalion
10	Church parade in the village in conjunction with artillery
11	Bde practiced attack 6th Northamptonshire right assaulting Battalion
12	Wet day : parades cancelled.
13	Bde. practiced attacks in presence of 2nd Corps commander 6th Northamptonshire Regiment 4th Battalion

CANCHY

14	Battalion moved to CANCHY. Bde. Schools of Bombing, Signalling, Trench Mortars established

Near a huge wood called the Crecy Forest and it's nice to walk under cover of trees, even if they have no leaves. I feel protected and hearing the birds singing makes me feel free but deep in my mind I'm still nervous and I spring into protective mode at any unusual sound. If anything the quietness works against me.

Here I am, totally used to the sounds of the trenches but when a twig breaks, I jump like a bloody scared rabbit. Still, I'll get over it in time.

I'm not sure how to act with the new lads. They're so innocent and full of enthusiasm and us old timers don't want to tell them the reality. We want them to remain innocent but we want them to become adult and understand what they'll be going into.

I feel like a father to them and I want to protect them but I also realise that I need to leave them to discover the real world. I'm not enjoying the feelings because I'm helpless to protect them.

We sit around the fire laughing and joking and the new lads think we're exaggerating our stories. When they get up and walk away I picture Alfy, with all his hope and innocence. It hurts so much because I don't want to think of him having to experience this, but I do. It's doubly hard because I can't let it show.

15   Company training. Last two drafts drilling under R.S.M and special instructions

16   Company Training. Range finally completed, with gallery, for firing
      2Lt LLOYD, joined on the 13th, posted to A Coy –

17   Church parade on football ground

Why can't I get the Christmas feeling? Life just seems to be the same, day in, day out. I need to talk to the lads about making some decorations and a party hat and hope that will spark the fire.

      Military Cross awarded to 2 Lts Higham, Bates and Gotch

18.   Company Training : junior N.C.O.s class under C.S.M's

19   Company Training : junior N.C.O.s class under C.S.M's
      a/Capt UNWIN proceeded to 5th Army School
      Bayonet Fighting Course for senior N.C.Os under a Staff Sergt Major for 6 days

20.   Company Training -

21.   Company Training

22   Inspection of Division at training by 5th Army Commander 6th
      Northamptonshire Regiment not visited

After all the preparation for the Army Commander's visit, he didn't come; bloody typical.

I was right, talking to the lads, preparing Christmas decorations and making little party hats from old newspapers sparked the spirit and now that they're finished, I think they're quite good, if I say so myself.

23   Company Training

24   No church parade : voluntary services

Happy Wedding Anniversary my love. Sixteen happy years of marriage that have given us great memories and loving children. Wish I could be there with you and the kids. We would have such a celebration with laughing and dancing and lots of food and drink with George, Kate and the kids.

I'm feeling a bit down not being there with you Trudy so I'll go to the Christmas Service to see if it'll make me feel any better; really miss you my love.

25   Christmas dinners in two relays. A & B at 12 noon. C and D at 2.30 p.m. Church parade at 9.45.

Well, I must admit, I do feel better having sung a few hymns while thinking of you and the kids my love. My mind was everywhere and with everyone as I was singing. Really bucked me up and the other good news is that we're on the first relay for Christmas dinner – should get the best scoff.

It would be so lovely now to hear Irchester Church bells ringing out. I wonder what presents Trudy got for the kids. Not feeling so nice, a bit lonely really; surrounded by pals but totally alone.

Here I am, sitting with hundreds of men wearing silly home-made hats and eating the Army's version of Christmas dinner. I suppose, taking into consideration the conditions, the turkey doesn't taste too bad and it's sheer luxury after a year of bully beef and biscuits.

Everybody's laughing, joking and singing and you wouldn't think we're in the middle of a life and death existence – life's really, really strange – it's just not real.

I wish you and the kids a wonderful day my love – Happy Christmas my love and may we have many more in happier times.

I'm feeling better but I'm not.

26   Battalion marched over to BUIGNY-ST-MACLOU for Divisional Gymkhana.

Apart from having a day off so I could play with the kids, I've never really liked Boxing Day much. That said, it was a nice show today and it was doubly nice to stroke and hug the horses. Their texture and smells bring back happy childhood memories of the ploughing and harvesting seasons in Astcote.

We think we have it hard, but these poor buggers haven't a clue of why all this is going on – all they can do is suffer in silence – poor buggers. I wish I could do something for them.

Ah well, Christmas is over for another year; let's hope I see another one. If I make it, I'll make sure Trudy and the kids have an extra special one next year – that is, if this bloody war is over.

27	54th Bde demonstrated attack before G.O.C. 5th Army and Divn and Bde Staffs of 2nd Corps : 6th Northamptonshire Regt. 4th Battalion.
28	Company Training
29.	Company Training . Information received that Director of Artillery – War Office has noted three German Machine Guns as captured by the 6th Northamptonshire Regt.
30.	Company Training.
31.	Church Parade at 10.30 a.m.

<u>S.H. Charrington</u> Lt Col
Commanding 6th Northamptonshire Regt.

OPERATIONS ON THE ANCRE

CANCHY
Jan 1917

Happy New Year?! What's there to be so bloody happy about?! We're still here, the war's still here and we're still training to kill people. All because one guy got shot. All these people dead because of one guy. Where's the reasoning?! Why can't they just see reason and call a halt to all this?!

Christ, I need to calm down. New Year's Day is the same as Boxing Day for me, if it wasn't for the kids, I'd cancel the days. Go and have a brew with the lads Bob and think happy thoughts of Trudy and the kids safely tucked up in peaceful Irchester.

1. Company training
2. Company training. Short Bn parade at 12:45 a.m. for arms drill etc. Messages wishing Bn Good Luck in coming year received from 1st, 2nd, 5th & 7th Bns.
3. Bn route march.

I quite like route marching. It gets us out to see different places and it gives us time to think of nice things. There's no bloody cracks, thuds and explosions, the air is fresh and it gives a rhythm to life.

4. Company training. Increase in establishment of Lewis Gunners commenced.
5. Company training. Bn had baths.
6. The Bn was fitted with the new Box Respirator. Bde cross country race won by Sgt BRADBURY.
7. Church parade 11 a.m. Received Gazette with New Year Honours.
   D.S.O. Lt. Col. S H Charrington.
   Mentioned in Despatches.
   Ripley Lt Col & Hon Col G.E.
   Charrington Capt. (Temp. Maj) S. H.   Res. of Off. Hns.
   Podmore Temp. Maj. H. D.S.O.
   Neville Temp Capt F.S.
   Beasley Temp Lt J.N.
   Bates Temp 2 Lt G.C.

Gotch Temp 2 Lt D.I.

Fowler Temp. QM & Hon Lt. WH.

Carters Nº 13166 Com QM Sgt R.J.

Bradbury Nº 14455 Sgt C.

Leatherland Nº 14625 Sgt F.R.

Mmmmmmmmmmmm, New Year's Honours. None for the likes of us common Privates. No medals or honours for me in 1916 but I have the reward of luck. I'm still alive and in one piece and that, in itself, is a huge medal.

When I come to think about it, what a hell of a year, literally. In 1915, I was a boot maker living a normal and free family life in Irchester with no grudge against anybody. In 1916, through no fault of my own, I'm ripped from my family to travel to another country and kill people who I have no grudge against.

Here I am in 1917, still following orders because, if I don't, my own kind will shoot me.

Inside, I'm still the same man I was in 1915 but I now have no peace, no rhythm and no freedom. I've been turned from a happy family man into a devoid of emotion killer. Christ, what a situation I'm in; the only way out is to stay alive.

8. Company training
9. Company training. At 10:0 a.m. Major General Maxse said goodbye to the Bde at Bde HQ. There was no formal parade but each Bn was represented by those officers who had served with the Bde longest & knew the Divisional Commander best. At the same time General Maxse presented decorations to all those who had had them awarded but had not been presented with them.
10 Kit inspection and cleaning up in preparation to move.
11. The Bde commenced its march into forward area. The Bn moved to billets in DOMQUEUR.

DOMQUEUR

12. March continued. Bn moved to billets in FIENVILLERS.

FIENVILLERS

13. Day spent in resting.

We've been here before. Came from another direction but my gut feeling on our way down was right, we've travelled this road before.

14. March continued. Bn moved to billets in RUBEMPRE. A trying march over bad roads. On several occasions the Bn had to march in single file. Advance party went from RUBEMPRE to the line by bus.

Not a good day for the feet but it got us ready for the trenches. Remember Bob, don't be a hero, get yourself back to Trudy and the kids.

In the LINE

15. The Bn took over line from 2/8th Bn R War.R in right   1/20,000 57° S.E. sector of Bde front. Bn front extended from W. MIRAUMONT RD on right to about R.16.c.65. The Bn left RUBEMPRE by bus at 9:30 am and arrived at AVELUY at 2:0 pm where the men had dinners. Relief was complete about midnight.

As we came out of Albert along what I understand to be the Roman Road, we were told we were about a mile from one of the bloody great explosions we heard on the 1st July last year. It just doesn't seem right that in all this time, after 6 months, we're still sitting and fighting on roughly the same front line.

Still, here we are again, in the trenches and here we go again, keeping the bloody rats at bay and ducking and diving between the cracks, thuds and explosions but I must admit, it's quite quiet for the front line. Perhaps the weather's keeping the enemy's hands in their pockets because that's where mine are. Brew time me thinks...

16. Frost getting more severe. A quiet day practically no shelling.

17. The formation adopted by 2/8th R War R was not considered satisfactory and the following dispositions were substituted. A Coy on right, B Coy on left in front line (DESIRE). This line held by a succession of posts; there is no continuous trench.

What a place, just a shallow hole in the ground and it's not at all comfortable with it being so bloody cold. We can't move around so we just have to snuggle up against each other to keep ourselves warm.

        Each of these Coys has two supporting platoons in REGINA TRENCH. C Coy in HESSIAN TRENCH as counter attack Coy and D Coy in ZOLLERN trench as reserve Coy. This arrangement was carried out at night without incident. 2 Lt. Higham went out on patrol and gained useful information regarding enemy defences.

18   Very quiet all day. Frost getting more severe. Three slight casualties.

Shit, I'm cold and I'm having trouble keeping the circulation in my feet. I can't keep drinking tea to keep warm because the cold's got my kidneys and it's bloody uncomfortable relieving myself.

19   Very quiet all day. On morning of 20th C.O. 2nd in Command & two front line Com Commanders carried out a reconnaissance with a view to moving some of the posts into more advantageous positions.

20   The Bn was relieved by the 11th Bn Royal Fusiliers. The relief was reported all complete by 10:30 pm. The Bn took over WARWICK HUTS vacated by the 11th Royal Fusiliers. Frost very intense and duckboards very slippery coming out. C Coy left in line attached to the 11th Royal Fusiliers.

If the bombs and bullets don't get you, the duckboards will. What a life but then again, it's nice and warm in the huts and I do feel for the lads out there in the line. Ah well, enjoy the comfort while you can Bob.

21.   Inspections of kit etc. & cleaning up huts

22.   The Bn resting in huts. All Coys doing physical drill in the morning.

23.   The Bn resting in huts. The Lewis Gun Officer gave lectures in the huts.

Nice and cosy in the huts but all good things come to an end; off to relieve the 11^{ths} tomorrow so I need to write a letter. Happy birthday Mum; you would have been 62 today. Still miss your reassuring smile and hugs and the lovely memories of you teaching me to make daisy chains in the field at the back of our house in Astcote.

24   Preparation for move back into line.

Here we go, steady now. I can see the headlines – Robert Furness invalided out of the Army after falling on slippery duckboards.

        At night the Bn relieved the 11th Royal Fusiliers in the same sector.

        Relief reported complete by 8:30 pm in spite of very slippery duckboards.

Dispositions D Coy on right, C Coy on left in front line, B Coy counter attack Coy and A Coy Reserve Coy. Front line Coys put out all the trip wire available during the night.

Shit its bloody cold and the pain when you get a nip from the barbed wire or pinch you finger is bloody excruciating.

25. Shelling below normal. Frost very severe. 2Lt Higham went out on patrol at night but was forced to return owing to our own shells dropping short. RE material dumps established with both front line Coys.

26. Shelling below normal. Frost very severe. New RE material dump formed in REGINA TRENCH. "B" Coy reclaimed part of REGINA TRENCH and established fire positions. Two casualties owing to a man lifting a dud shell with a pick.

What an idiot! Hitting a shell with a pick. I know there's a chance of your skin sticking to the frozen metal but there's other ways of moving a shell other than a pick; what an idiot!

The idea of small sandbags on the feet is a bloody good idea. Stops us slipping on the duckboards and they help insulate our feet from the frozen ground. I must say, there's some pretty smart people around here.

27. A quiet day. The Bn was relieved at night by the 8th Bn Suffolk Rgt. Relief reported all complete by 8:15 pm. The duckboards were very slippery but the men all had sandbags around their feet. The Bn took over MACKENZIE HUTS in W.10.C   1/20,000 57° S.E.

28 Rested in huts. Very cold.

Aaaaaaaah, the huts are nice and warm and cosy, relatively speaking. This war does have some good points.

29. One and a half Coys on working party under R.E. ½ Coy working for Bde. ½ Coy cleaning up camp. Remainder cutting wood for the Bn in AUTHUILLE WOOD for burning purposes. Very little coke being issued. Untrained draft withdrawn from Coys and trained under Bn arrangements.

Cutting wood brings back great memories as a kid in Astcote, especially the cosy feeling and the smell of burning wood – lovely.

30	Working parties as yesterday. More wood cut. Training of draft continued. Bde conference for C.O. 2nd in Command & Adjt at Bde H.Q. Plans for proposed attack discussed. Baths for one Coy.

Bathing is bitter sweet in this weather. I'm not sure if the feeling clean bit warrants the unpleasantness of taking my clothes off in the freezing cold.

31	Working parties as yesterday. Baths for one Coy.

R J F Meyricks Lt Col.

1917
Feb
MᶜKENZIE HUTS

1. Working parties and baths. Practice in forming up, advancing & digging in on reverse slopes.
2. Same as Feb 1. Lt Col CHARRINGTON left the Battalion to take command of C Battⁿ Heavy Branch, Machine Gun Corps.
3. Lt Col R.J.F. MEYRICKE (of the 11ᵗʰ Royal Fusiliers) assumed command. Working parties and practice attacks.
4. Working parties by night only.

Happy Birthday my love, 38 today. Not working by day gives me the time to think of you and wonder what the children have done for you. I suppose you've been making a nice dinner for everybody or are you combining your and Annie's birthday treats together? I hope the weather's sunny and not too cold and it cheers you up my love. Love and miss you so much.

5. As for Feb 4

Happy Birthday Annie. It's events such as this that you and I will be thinking of each other across the miles and wishing we could have a lovely long cuddle to make us both feel safe. I love you my child.

So, 14 years old and I bet you are a lovely young lady now. I wonder if you have a favourite boy or if you're playing with your friends today; probably both. I wonder what you're doing now but I picture you walking around the village feeling free as a bird with great expectations. I also feel that you're thinking of me and wishing me a speedy journey home. Happy Birthday my child, enjoy your day.

Time for a brew...

6. Three companies practiced forming up, advancing & digging in on reverse slopes

I'm a boot and shoe man, not a miner and killer.

7. 4 companies working on new divisional tramway. OVILLERS: Ground frozen two feet down: work very slow
8. As for Feb 7

Christ its cold; when will the weather turn and allow Spring to arrive? Actually, come to think of it, although it's hard work digging this frozen ground it keeps us warm and out of harm's way. Also, when the weather warms up, the bullets and explosions will start again so just enjoy the season Bob.

9   As for Feb 8: companies went up in drill order, packs brought up by transport to WARWICK HUTS, where the battalion moved in the afternoon.

WARWICK HUTS

10   Two companies on working parties: remainder Coy organisation.

11   As for Feb 10

12   4 companies working on new divisional tramway to RIFLE DUMP 7:30 to 12 relieved by 2 Coys 12th Middlesex & 2 Coys 11th Royal Fusiliers. Battalion moved to GLOSTER HUTS in the afternoon.

GLOSTER HUTS

13   Work on tramway : two companies 8:15a.m. to 12:30 p.m. two companies 12:30 p.m. to 4:45 p.m.

14   As for Feb 13th & baths in afternoon.

Valentine's Day. I wonder how many women are thinking of their loved ones today? Happy Valentine's Day my Trudy and sorry, no flowers to pick for you here.

TRENCHES

15   Battalion took over its battlefront from the 8th Bn East Surry Regt. v. Appendix

16   Preparations for battle : forming up positions marked out by 12 midnight: first company reached GULLY at 1 a.m.

17   Battle forming up completed by 5 a.m. v Appendix R Turner Lt. Colonel

Well here we go George, another day in the life of an infantryman; Happy Birthday brother – I'll have a cup of tea to celebrate your day after we've finished with this attack. Luckily, we're in Reserve.

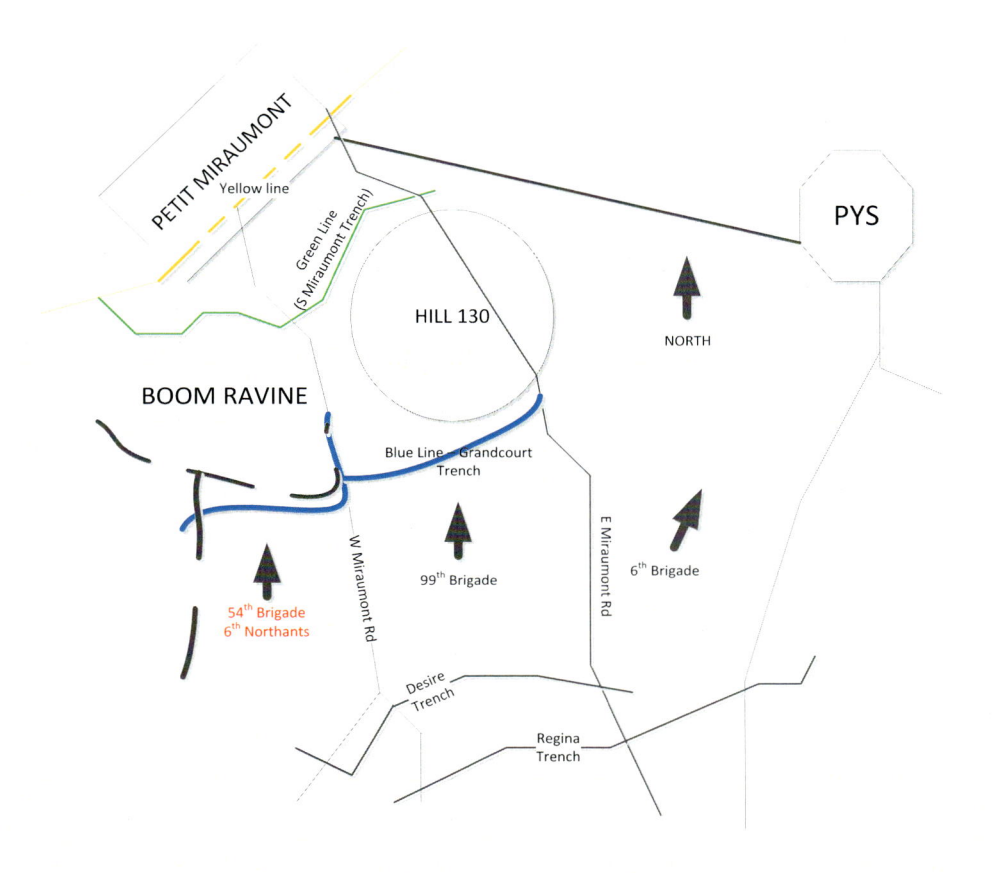

Narrative of the part played by the 6th Northamptonshire Regiment
in the operations against S. MIRAUMONT TRENCH Feb: 17 1917

On the night of Feb: 15 the Battalion took over the battle front from the 8th East Surry Regiment. This front was held by one Company, the others being situated as shown in the Appendix.

The front was carefully reconnoitred for forming-up lines but no actual marks were put in on the night of the 15th. At about 5 am, the enemy opened a fairly heavy barrage on the line of the GULLY & 80 yards north of it.

This was most useful – enabling us to adjust our forming and positioning & closing them up, so as to have all lines well clear of the GULLY where it seemed his barrage would come.

On the night of the 16th 2Lt BOULTON (O.C. B Company holding the line) & 2Lt HIGHAM (Intelligence Officers assisted by officers & N.C.O.s of the assaulting companies got the lines for forming up taped out & otherwise marked & our own wire sufficiently cut by 12 midnight. They accomplished this in spite of great difficulties owing to the extreme darkness of the night & although a heavy enemy barrage was opened on them at about 9 p.m.

 Orders had been received that all troops were to be in position by 4:45 a.m. i.e. an hour before the time fixed for zero hour.

 At 1 a.m. the leading platoon of C Company (the left assault company) reached the GULLY and was at once taken out to its position by guides. There was some congestion on the way up at the time and the rest of the company with its attached dug-out clearing parties was not in position till nearly 2:30. However, at 3:30 the whole of A Company, the centre company, was also in position with its dug-out clearing parties. by 4:15 the leading 3 platoons of the right company (D) were also in position : just before 4:30 however as the last platoon with Coy H.Q. & Lewis Guns were being taken out into position the enemy sent up yellow & green light sprays & a heavy barrage was immediately opened on the line of the GULLY & a line measuring about 80 yards N. of it. This last platoon of D Company suffered heavy casualties from these shells – the whole of one Lewis Gun team becoming casualties & the O.C. Company, Capt. Unwin being slightly wounded & suffering a serious concussion. The acting sergeant major however showed splendid coolness : got the platoon together again & placed them in their forming-up positions.

 The shelling while the 4th company was moving into its position N.E. of the GULLY about 4:45 a.m. was extremely heavy & there were a certain amount of casualties : too high praise cannot be given to 2 Lt BOULTON and C.S.M. CUTHBERT for their courage & coolness in directing the move under these trying circumstances.

 The whole battalion was in position by 4:50 a.m. The enemy shelling continued heavy till 5:30 a.m. & then slackened a little. It was afterwards discovered that the enemy had received information of the attack 6 hours previously from some deserters (or prisoners) from the Division on the right, who had told them everything except that they put the zero hour at 5:15 instead of 5:45. The barrage was certainly much heavier than in the previous morning & was on this occasion accompanied by S.O.S signals in great profusion.

The morning was extremely dark (heavy clouds obscuring the moon which should have risen about 4:20 a.m.) the ground was very soft and slippery – the thaw after nearly a month's hard frost having just commenced & altogether conditions could not have been more unfavourable to forming-up for an attack absolutely without trenches.

The greatest credit is due to 2 Lt's BOULTON & HIGHAM for the success of the forming up and to all ranks for the absolute quiet & order with which the forming up was carried out & the calm courage with which they lay on the mud (some of them for 3 or 4 hours) with this heavy hostile shelling upon them. Actual casualties among the lines actually formed up & lying down were extremely few but the test of discipline was extremely severe.

At 5:45 a.m. our barrage opened & the enemy at once sent up showers of yellow spray lights & some green lights as well. His answering barrage was however very short lived & it would seem that our counter-battery work on this morning was excellent.

Our men had no difficulty in following our barrage up to GRANDCOURT TRENCH – though the light was very poor until after 6 a.m. but on arrival at the wire they found in many cases that it had not been cut. Only a few very narrow passages were to be found & the delay in finding these gave the enemy time to get into position again both in GRANDCOURT TRENCH & also on both sides of the BOOM RAVINE. This movement along the wire to find gaps was also largely responsible for the loss of direction & mixing up of companies which took place in the case of the left company (C) the first two waves & those behind were held up by machine gun & rifle fire in GRANDCOURT TRENCH, which delayed them at least half an hour & caused heavy casualties. The O.C. Company Lt WINKWORTH & another Officer 2Lt COOPER both became casualties before getting over GRANDCOURT TRENCH.

The front two waves of the ~~enthst~~ centre company (A) got over GRANDCOURT TRENCH with little opposition but were then met by heavy machine gun & trench mortar fire from their left, a large body of Germans holding the tongue in the BOOM RAVINE about R.11.C.5.3. It was necessary to clear this point before advancing : during this operation A/CAPT M^{c}WHA & Lt HERIZ-SMITH being casualties. The rear waves of the centre company met with considerable opposition in GRANDCOURT TRENCH. It is not clear whether this opposition was present when the first two waves went through or not but the 4th wave encountered machine guns in the wire of GRANDCOURT TRENCH.

The right company D was the only one which was able to advance from BOOM RAVINE in anything like time for the barrage – that is to say half an hour after entering it. The left & centre companies were occupied for a good hour in clearing GRANDCOURT trench and the RAVINE : no actual time is available - only one company officer ~~ngdrtg~~ surviving crossed the RAVINE – but it seems quite certain that none of the left or centre company started out of the RAVINE till a clear half hour after the barrage had lifted from its first halt. Of the right company a certain number – chiefly those who losing direction - had moved ~~also~~ so as to leave BOOM RAVINE just as their left did, after finding their mistakes & regaining direction start up the hill in R.11.C on the W. of the West MIRAUMONT road. But even these only arrived in time to see the barrage leaving the top of the hill & by the time they came in view of SOUTH MIRAUMONT trench, the barrage was on the N side of it & Germans already re-appearing in the trench. The 2nd Division on our right had established themselves in positions on S MIRAUMONT trench : our men found only a very few gaps cut in the wire & was forced in the majority of cases to lie down first on our side of the wire & try and cut it. Later a few parties one under 2/Lt HIGHAM MC & the others under Lt PRICE did enter the trench W of W MIRAUMONT road and establish a footing. But on the whole the number of 18th Divisional troops in SOUTH MIRAUMONT trench was small : whereas the trench E of W MIRAUMONT road was fairly thickly occupied of British troops.

It was at this time – apparently about 8:30 a.m. that is to say when our Barrage was behind the 3rd objective – that a strong German counter attack was delivered from PETIT MIRAUMONT & the GULLY in R 5 d. This appears to have been the main attack though parties also advanced from the banks in R 5 C (on the GRANDCOURT – MIRAUMONT roads). It appears from captured German orders & statements of prisoners, that these were specially trained counter-attack troops, who had been brought up as soon as the information of our coming attack reached them on the preceding night: they consisted largely of marksmen and machine gunners. The fire was extremely accurate, while in the majority of cases the British rifles & Lewis & Vickers Guns had become clogged almost from the start – owing to them lying in the mud in the dark before the attack & the bad ground traversed during the advance.

 Whatever the exact cause, the British line seeing no appreciable effect provided by their fire on the advancing Germans began to fall back chiefly on the right & then all along the line. It was at this point that Lt PRICE (Adjutant of the 6th Northamptonshire's) displayed most conspicuous gallantry. He moved to & fro along the line – steadying the retirement. Then perceiving that our right was being left in the air & thinking our left comparatively safe, he formed the whole Northampton body of survivors into a defensive flank on the W MIRAUMONT road. This was done by him personally under heavy rifle & machine gun fire & done most successfully. In this position they stayed from about 9 to 9:30: at this time fire began to be opened on them from their left rear i.e. from S MIRAUMONT trench – with both machine guns & light trench mortars. After suffering many casualties for some time Lt PRICE decided to swing back his line & face his original front: this also was carried out under heavy fire & at about 10 a.m. the Batt[n] was occupying a line about 100 yards N of BOOM RAVINE.

 This position was maintained till the afternoon – when in conjunction with the 11th Royal Fusiliers the line was pushed forward almost to the crest of the hill & occupied by a series of rifle & machine gun posts.

 This line was handed over to the 8th East Surry Regiment on the evening of Feb 18th.

 A summary of casualties is attached. (could not be found in the War Diary)

H Podmore Major

April 5

MARLBOROUGH HUTS

Feb

18   Battalion relieved by company of 8th East Surry Regt. return to MARLBOROUGH HUTS.

I'm getting used to all this now, it's a case of getting into my skin bubble, going over the top and just following my automatic survival instincts. It's funny to think that I've just come back from an attack to kill people and it doesn't really bother me anymore. I'm not even concerned about the hell the other guys have just gone through – it wasn't my fight.

There's no sense or rhythm anymore, it's just a case of following orders, helping each other to survive and coming back for a rest and a brew.

Hmmm, a brew; good idea. Tea with a hint of petrol while I think about George's birthday and a few thoughts for John Jeffries and Fred Luck who won't be going back to the village ever again. They're the 2nd and 3rd of my village mates from the Battalion not to make it – John and Fred, a day after each other; not good.

Not nice for the Postman delivering the telegrams either. It was an honour to have met you, so steadfast in all we did together. Thank you for being there for me. I'll go and see your families when I get back and tell them how well you fought and what good friends you were.

BOUZINCOURT

19   Battalion moved to billets in BOUZINCOURT : message of congratulation from Brigadier on the recent operations – more than upholding the reputation of the 54th Bde.

Things don't seem to be progressing well because they don't seem to be moving us far from the front lines just north-west of Albert these days.

20   Baths and refitting

Mmmmmmmmm, this water's nice and warm. The last bash wasn't too bad for us in reserve but the other lads took a hell of a beating. Apparently we did well and I get this feeling that the tide's beginning to turn in our favour. Perhaps the end's in sight and I'll soon be back home strolling over the fields and following the brook between the Sluice and

Green Lane; I love that stretch of water. Aaaaaaaaah, thiiiis baaaaaaaaaath's niiiiiiiiiiiiiiiiice...

21   Messages of congratulations to the Division from the Corps and Army Commanders. Organisation & drill

22   Organisation and drill on ground N. of BOUZINCOURT. Congratulations from C in C.

THE GERMAN RETREAT TO THE HINDENBURG LINE

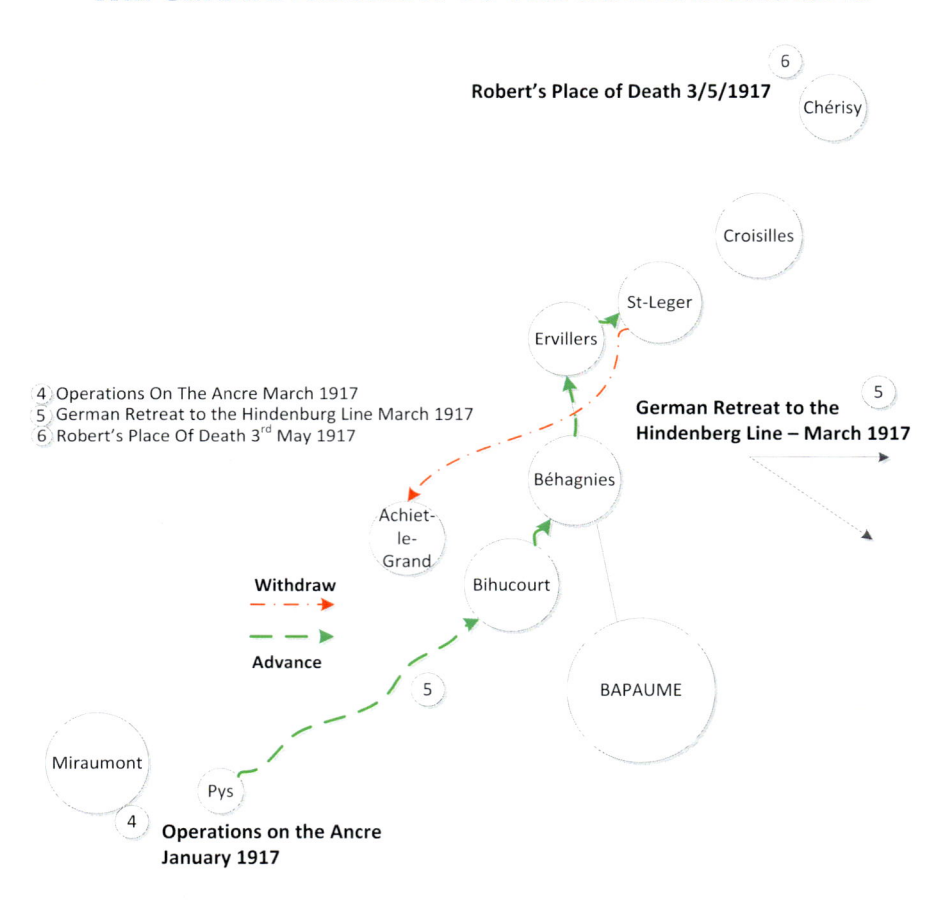

Robert's Place of Death 3/5/1917

Chérisy

Croisilles

St-Leger

Ervillers

4) Operations On The Ancre March 1917
5) German Retreat to the Hindenburg Line March 1917
6) Robert's Place Of Death 3rd May 1917

German Retreat to the Hindenberg Line – March 1917

Béhagnies

Achiet-le-Grand

Withdraw

Bihucourt

Advance

BAPAUME

Miraumont

Pys

Operations on the Ancre January 1917

BOUZINCOURT

Feb

23   One coy working in ENGLEBELMER road : remainder training

24   Two coys working in ENGLEBELMER road: remainder training – in the special instructions in box respirator.

25   Church Parade in the CINEMA at 11 a.m. No working parties. Lt & Adjt T.R. Price proceeded on a fortnight's special leave

Nice quiet day today. Bit of a sing song at the parade and then messing about and doing nothing over a brew. We should have more days like this...

26   Coy. parades for bombing – musketry, etc. on ground N. of BOUZINCOURT.

27   Coy. parades as on 26. In the afternoon battalion passed through a gas-cloud to demonstrate the efficiency of the box-respirator if properly fitted. One slight casualty through badly fitted mask –

That wasn't nice at all. The thought of knowing you're going to get gassed isn't nice at all.

My stomach was grumbling in sympathy with my fear as I fastened every button to cover every bit of exposed skin and then there was the claustrophobia as I put my respirator on. The ringing in my ears gave it another dimension as if my head was in a fish bowl.

It was frightening and funny all at the same time. I felt as though they were taking the piss out of us because we were just standing there and not really feeling anything but reality suddenly burst through as one of the guys started jumping around like a startled rabbit. Apparently he didn't fit his respirator correctly and a bit of gas got in... must ask him how it felt.

Even after you come out of the test area you're covered in residue and although you're warned not to touch your clothes and skin for a while, it's virtually impossible not to do so. The burning, even with the slightest brush on the skin, leaves you in no doubt as to the horrors of the affects the gas can have on you before you die. I remember thinking, I must go and change because that's not nice stuff at all but at least it's comforting to know the respirators work.

28   Coy. parades for bombing – musketry & physical drill – extended orders.

R Turner Lt. Colonel

BOUZINCOURT

March

1 Company parades for musketry, bombing and Rifle Range –Major Turner D.S.O. assumed command of the battalion

THIEPVAL WOOD

2 Battalion moved to dug-outs and tents in THIEPVAL WOOD

Aaaah, under canvas on ground that I helped to capture – nice warm feeling of having achieved something.

Being out in the wild away from civilisation, nice. Bit ironic really because the wilds are woods that are smashed to pieces, there's no wildlife apart from the rats and lice and this devastation has to be considered as 1917 civilisation.

With it still being a bit nippy, the tents give a feeling of being warm, snug and protected and it gives me a warm glow.

3 Coy parades & inspection by Commanding Officer
4 250 men working parties on GRANDCOURT, MIRAUMONT road – remainder drill. musketry, bombing : Lewis Gun classes
5 Working parties as on 4th : parades as before for remainder
6 Working parties : parades for remainder: NCOs under Army Gymnastic Instructor

Sometimes, being a nothing has its advantages. I'm quite happy just working my muscles with everyday work; no gymnastics for an old timer like me.

7 Two companies working party, remainder firing range & live bombing in trenches near THIEPVAL : NCOs under Army Gymnastic Instructor
8 Working parties, parades as before Lt & Q'Mr W H FOWLER left the battalion to take up duties at G.H.Q. as Instructor in Catering. Drafts of 50 and 92 men
9 Training and working parties as before
10 Training and working parties as before. Award of 13 Military Medals & 4 Bars to Military Medals for NCOs & men for the operations against S MIRAUMONT Trench.

In a bit of a routine with all this training and working parties but at least we're not being shot at. Still no medal but what the heck, apart from my ears, I'm still alive and in one piece.

11   Practice attack against ACHIET-LOUPART line on ground near AUTHUILLE. Battery in morning

Ah, the bombardment has started so it looks like we're off to the front line again. It's a pity the real stuff isn't like the practice attacks.

News came in that William Needham from the village was killed yesterday. My thoughts are with you Bill, I hope it was quick.

12   Battⁿ relieved units of the 53rd Infantry Brigade – taking over their battle front for the ACHIET-LOUPART attack. Very long arduous relief owing to distance, bad state of roads & fact of relieving 3 different units.

13   ACHIET-LOUPART line reported evacuated on our Right early in morning. Patrol under Sgt FRITZ discovered line opposite Battⁿ evacuated about 8 a.m.

B & C Companies advanced through ACHIET-LOUPART line & on to a line running from G.22.a.6.3 to G.22.c.8.1 with 12th Middlesex on right and 7th Bedford's on left.

With all these lads on the move there's hardly any room for us in these trenches. I believe we're moving north-east but it's difficult to keep my bearings.

I wonder how many of this sea of featureless faces will be alive tomorrow.

ACHIET LE PETIT still occupied. A Company in ACHIET line. Heavy enemy shelling on ACHIET line, IRLES, & forward of ACHIET line but very few casualties. Bⁿ H.Q. in GREVILLERS TRENCH.

14   Battⁿ relieved in front line in early morning by Middlesex & Bedford's B & C Companies in ACHIET line. A Coy in GREVILLERS line and IRLES : D Coy in S MIRAUMONT trench : Bⁿ H.Q. at PYS

15   No movement ACHIET LE PETIT still occupied.
PYS

16   No movement : enemy shelling still heavy in BIHUCOURT Line –

17   Early morning of 17th patrols of 12th Middlesex found BIHUCOURT line unoccupied & moved forward into BIHUCOURT which they occupied but were unable to emerge from the village owing to sniper & machine guns –

Well, we seem to be making good headway and capturing a lot of ground but it seems a bit too easy. It's as though they're retreating.

There's nothing left but rubble, even the trees have been chopped down. Every bridge and every building has been destroyed and they've left signs taunting us to try and use anything. How can civilised people become so uncivilised?

BIHUCOURT

17   Batt^n concentrated by mid-day in G 28 C : moved forward in evening to BIHUCOURT line 1 gun pit on South side of it.

18   Battalion moved as advance guard to Division – with two troops of cavalry & a section of field guns & occupied without opposition the BAPAUME - ARRAS road from ERVILLERS to BÉHAGNIES. ~~Altered~~ Cavalry gained trench into the evening on the hill between ERVILLERS & ST LEGER

We're making constant headway to the north-east towards a place called Arras, or something like that – can never really tell if we're saying the name right after it's passed through the grapevine of Northamptonshire dialect. Still, the Bosche seem to be backing off quite fast.

The tide's changing, I can feel it...

ERVILLERS

19   Battalion moved forward with a squadron of cavalry & a company of cyclists to occupy ST LEGER. This was only accomplished finally late in the afternoon. Trench was established with 2nd Division on the ST LEGER - MORY road & with 7th Division - by cavalry porters - at JUDAS FM

ST LEGER

19   Battalion held an outpost line on both sides of the valley running from ST LEGER to CROISILLES, on the Northern edge of ST LEGER

20 Battalion made a reconnaissance in force assisted by cavalry on both flanks – the LUCKNOW Brigade having also come up as the Corps cavalry – at 7:30 a.m. Four companies in line A. B. D. C from right to left. A Coy were unable to emerge from the wood at the N.E. corner of ST LEGER owing to heavy shelling & machine gun fire & suffered considerable casualties.

B Coy worked up the valley & dislodging an advanced post of the enemy made considerable progress in spite of heavy shelling.

Killing, killing, killing. There's nowhere to hide, lads are being shot and blown to pieces but still we move forward; death everywhere.

C & D Corps advanced on the slope N.W. of the valley but after going 400 or 500 yards came under heavy machine gun fire as well as considerable shelling.

At about 10:30 a.m. it was seen that CROISILLES was too strongly occupied to make any further advance – considering the wire in front of it & the fact that we were supported by only our battery R.F.A & one battery R.H.A – practicable. Orders were given for companies to withdraw to their original outpost positions.

Withdraw?! After all this?! Are they mad?! This isn't real! All those lads, dead; what for?! What have I just stumbled over; sorry mate, here grab my arm and hurry, lean on me but keep your head down. Careful Bob, careful, zigzag, zigzag, don't be an easy target.

This was done in perfect order & all companies were back by about 12:30 except about 40 men of D Company who were in a fold of ground – not visible from the front but not possible to emerge from in daylight. They decided to wait till dark.

However, about 4 p.m. a party of Germans came out from CROISILLES on their right & threatened to outflank them. They therefore came back in small parties without casualties – leaving, however one or two wounded men – These were recovered by the 8th Devon Regiment who relieved the Battalion that evening. Battalion proceeded to billets in ACHIET LE GRAND.

21   Battalion moved to WARWICK HUTS via duckboard trench from MIRAUMOUNT

Sitting here, my bubble's shrunk to my brain. Focused on nothing, utterly drained, ears ringing so, so loud, I just can't believe what we've been through. I thought I would be used to this by now but shit, I'm not. Christ, so many dead.

John Percival didn't make it - for what?! FOR WHAT?! He was such a great mate and all I can picture is his loving family walking about the village without him.

Shit, now I'm crying. It's not right, I haven't cried since Lucy Jane's death a couple of years ago. Christ, I don't know what to do. How long can I last? When will I finally crack? Will I crack?

Am I fighting to stay alive or to kill all I can so that this bloody war will end sooner? What have I become?

WARLOY

22   Battalion moved to WARLOY, marching past Corps Commander at SENLIS

Feeling better now thanks to the lad's help. My second family; a good bunch ready with a laugh and a joke. Moving in the right direction away from the killing helps.

It's surprising how quickly we accept and recover but are we accepting and recovering or just storing it up somewhere in the back of our minds?

Marching helps; the rhythm allowing the mind to wander freely through millions of transitory thoughts.

VILLERS BOCAGE

23   Battalion moved to VILLERS BOCAGE

24   Battalion moved by bus from VILLERS BOCAGE to DURY

News is filtering through that there's been a revolution in Russia and their Tsar Nicholas has abdicated. Apparently he's a relative of our King and those lads are on our side.

What the hell's going to happen now? If they give up, the Bosche will be able to move all their troops back towards us and we'll again feel the

full force – this war just isn't looking good...and there I was, thinking that we were beginning to win.

DURY

25 Church parade & company inspections by C.O.

These church parades take my mind off reality and help me relax. I definitely feel better afterwards. Perhaps there's some truth in the healing powers of Christ but what about the rest of the story; why would he allow this slaughter to happen?

I have no answers but at least I feel a bit better. News is that we're off up north towards Dunkerque way and even better news is that we're in for a train ride.

26 Battalion left DURY at 8:30 p.m. to entrain at BACOUEL (two hours march)

27 Battalion entrained about 5 a.m. & moved from BACOUEL Station at 7:15 a.m.

28 Battalion out-trained at BERGUETTE Station at about 7 a.m. and marched to billets at THIENNES

Three days of train journeys; nice but nice to get off and stretch the legs. You can only play cards for so long and sleeping wasn't easy; it was more cat naps between the nightmares.

THIENNES

29 Training for all Companies in bombing, bayonet fighting, etc. Guard monitoring under assistant adjutant.

Well here we are my Lily, happy 9th Birthday. I miss you terribly and I bet you've grown into a lovely young girl. I can imagine you laughing and dancing with your friends in Irchester; love you and looking forward so much to giving you a cuddle.

The thought of coming home to your mum and playing with you in the fields, gives me strength and keeps me going. Happy Birthday Lily.

30 Training as above. Message of appreciation from 5th Army Commander to 18th Division on leaving his army

We're in a nice place near a big forest called Nieppe, after the canal that skirts its edge.

The first signs of Spring make me feel good. Nothing should make me feel good with the state of the world but seeing nature marching on and rebuilding gives me strength and a sense of hope.

31   Training as above

R Turner Lt Colonel
6th Bn Northamptonshire Regt.

THIENNES

1/4/17 11 a.m. Church parade in square all units Bde

    9 a.m. Inspection of kit. The blankets of 2 Corps and transport were sterilized during the day

April Fool's Day and feeling good. Must keep my wits about me for the odd joke here and there.

What could be better than a Sunday morning lay-in, the sound of birdsong, the closeness of the forest and the relative calm that singing good old hymns does for you; said a prayer for Lucy Jane – it just seemed right.

2/4/17 Company training.

    9 a.m. Thorough Kit inspection. One Coys kit inspected by the C.O. Small Box Respirators tested.

Back to work – two Sundays in a row would have been nice.

3/4/17 10 a.m. Battalion route march. Training of Lewis Gunners continues.

    Musketry lecture by Capt. R W Roberts to officers and N.C.O.s

Two years my child; it's been two years since you passed away my Lucy Jane. Time has flown by and my world has changed beyond words since Pneumonia took you from us.

If the world continues like this, you're in a better place. I'm feeling very sad but I must put it to the back of my mind and remember the lovely times we had together while you were with us. Such a lovely innocent and happy girl; you made us very happy and for that I thank you. Rest in peace my child.

4/4/17 Company training. Lecture to Coy by Major Podmore on map reading

5/4/17 Coy training. Coys used rifle range during the day

6/4/17 Coy training. C.O's inspections of organisation of all Coys during the day

Been told that the Americans have declared war on Germany. More innocents to the slaughter. They've no idea what they're letting themselves in for. Yes, I'm pleased that more support is coming but it means that the end's not in sight; what bitter sweet news.

7/4/17 Coy training. training of 2 Coys rifle grenades under Bombing Officer.

    Medical Officer's inspection of feet

8/4/17 Church parade, Presentation of medal ribbons decorations etc. granted in connection with recent operations on the SOMME by the Corps Commander. Military Cross Lt J.N. Beasley Lt G Kemp R.A.M.C att to Bn. Military Medals 9 other ranks Bars to Military Medal 4 other Ranks

More medals; what about the medals for those who have given their all for a few inches of ground! All I want is to stay alive and for this war to end; I don't need a medal.

They're giving them away like confetti to the Officers but what about us poor bastards who didn't want to come here; where's our rewards?!

Sing, Bob, sing; it's Easter and Spring is in the air. Think of Trudy and the kids and everything breaking out in flower in Irchester. Think of St. Katherine's Church bells ringing, think of the children playing and laughing in the fields; sing Bob, sing.

9/4/17 Coy training. Coys used range during the day
10/4/17 Battalion training (Outpost Scheme)

News just arrived and it's not good news at all. Three guys from the village were killed yesterday, Albert Clark, John George and John Sawford.

How must the messenger feel, cycling into the village to deliver telegrams to three distraught families who know the contents before they're even opened?

11/4/17 Muster Parades all Coys.   Coys used range during the day
12/4/17 Company training.
13/4/17 Battalion Route March (7 miles)

I'm feeling better now and the route march is helping. No need to think, just let the rhythm of the march take over. I hope it goes on all day, I need the rhythm and the time to resolve my inner demons.

14/4/17 Company training. Coys instructed in Bayonet fighting etc. by CSM Jones Army Gymnastics Staff during the day. Rifle parade sections of 2 Coys received instruction under Bombing Officer. Military Medal awarded to 5 other ranks. Bar to Military Medal to 1 other rank. Coys and Divisional Commdrs send congratulations to the recipients.
15/4/17 Baths at AIRE allotted to the Battalion all day. All Battn bathed.

Church parade for 2 Coys.

What a day. Even though we're surrounded by war, Spring's in the air. Singing and feeling clean helps tremendously.

16/4/17 Company training

17/4/17 Brigade Outpost scheme cancelled owing to wet weather

Instruction under Platoon Comdrs in billets. Preparations made for Bn Sports

18/4/17 Battn Sports cancelled owing to wet weather

Typical. The weather here's just as bad as back home. Now to try and stay awake during boring lectures.

Instruction (lectures etc.) by platoon Comdrs in billets

19/4/17 Battn Sports weather dull. Sports very satisfactory

Nobody gave a damn about the weather, the footy was good, even though we didn't win.

1st Line transport inspected by Col Grose 18th Div Trans.

20/4/17 Coy training

21/4/17 Battalion moved to MANQUEVILLE (new billets)

MANQUEVILLE

22/4/17 Church parade Voluntary Services during morning and evening

Enjoyed the singing today. Perhaps there's a bit of a performer in me. I must look into joining a choir or a stage act when I get back.

23/4/17 Battalion took part in Brigade Tactical Exercise (Outpost Scheme)

Not good news today about Russia – been informed that it's collapsed and under the control of some new leader called Lenin.

24/4/17 Company training. Muster parades for all Coys during the day (checking organisation)

25/4/17 Company training. Baths at LILLERS allotted to Bn all day. All Bn bathed

If the rest of the war's like this then I won't complain; a bath works wonders.

26/4/17 Brigade Tactical exercise cancelled owing to notice received that we were to be prepared to move any time after 1 p.m.

Battn moved to new billets at BOURS.

Christ, deep down, I knew yesterday's highs were too good to be true but it was nice to be in that state of mind for even a short time.

We've just been told to prepare for moving by one o'clock. Something drastic must have happened for such a rush order.

Harry Laughton from the village was killed yesterday and I'm not feeling good; too many highs and lows in such a short period of time.

BOURS

27.4.17 The Battn less transport were to entrain at PERNES for ARRAS at 10:30 a.m. but on arriving at PERNES at 9:20 a.m. information was received that owing to an accident on the railway in PERNES the battn were to march to BRYAS and entrain there.

Left PERNES and arrived at BRYAS at 2:40 p.m. and entrained for ARRAS. Arrived at ARRAS at 10:45 p.m., after being left waiting near the station for about 1½ hours. Marched to bivouacs at NEUVILLE-VITASSIE arriving there at about 1:45 a.m. 28.4.17

Although we're south of Arras again, they keep calling the area by the local river name of the Scarpe.

NEUVILLE-VITASSIE

28.4.17 Made arrangement to relieve the 2nd WILTS and 18 Kings Liverpools (30th Division) in the trenches (These two battns were not very strong). It was explained that we should take up the line (O.31.c.3) to 31.G.5.7 ref Map Sheet 51.G.S.W   Relief started at 8:15 p.m. and was complete at 1:10 pa.m. 29.4.17 There were no casualties. Weather fine.

Again, another little French village surrounded by wide open spaces and again, I suppose it would look lovely in peacetime.

A & D Coys in front line with C & B Coys in support. B Coy hold 2 strong points

At least the weather's nice and the rest was lovely. Must put the other world to the back of my mind and think solely of surviving. I can feel myself drawing back into my bubble as we move into the thick of it.

In the Trenches

29.4.17 A little shelling by the enemy of our trenches during the day

Lt ⌠ D.S Walker and 4 O.R. wounded (1 remained at duty)

Weather fine

30.4.17 Intermittent shelling all day. B Coy worked on digging trench on road from B Coy Hders to right of front line.

Funny really, here we are, digging a trench that the Bosche are trying their best to destroy; what a life hey?

C Coy worked on improving a long sap from front line from which good observation can be obtained.

Front line had to be extended to the left for 150 yards, 1 platoon of C Coy occupied this distance.

H Podmore Major
C of 6 Northamptonshire Regt

THE THIRD BATTLE OF THE SCARPE

In the trenches West of CHÉRISY

1.5.17 Weather fine. Quiet all day. Very little shelling.

From what I can make out, Croisilles is just south of us. It was here that we had to retreat a couple of months ago so we've only made about a mile of ground a month. Someday, I'll have to try and make some sense of all this.

2 Officers patrols went out at 9:30 p.m and returned at 11:30 pm. Right patrol reported that the enemy were not strong in their front line but judging from enemy very lights the trench further North was strongly held. On returning were fired at. No Casualties.

The Left patrol went along the CABLE TRENCH where they were held up by an enemy patrol. Shots were exchanged. No Casualties.

Later they went further – nothing to report.

The Battalion was relieved by the 12th MIDDLESEX Regiment and the 7th Bedford's and marched back to bivouacs at NEUVILLE VITASSE arriving there 2 ~~p.m~~ a.m. 2.5.17

Not nice but then again, not bad. A few shots here and there but not an area to worry about if we have to go back.

NEUVILLE VITASSE

2.5.17 Orders received that the Division would attack on a two Brigade front – the 54th on the right and the 55th Brigade on the Left. The 21st Division would attack on the right and the 14th Division on the left simultaneously. Objectives . blue and red lines . Map attached. Map was not attached

The Battalion were held in Brigade Reserve.

Preparations for battle made during the day. Only 20 Officers to go into action, the remainder to be with transport.

2 p.m. Conference of Officers held at Battalion Headquarters. Details explained.

3.5.17 Battalion left NEUVILLE VITASSE by Companies. 1st Company at

12:30 ~~p.m.~~ a.m. remaining Companies 5 minutes interval and marched to trenches at N.29.C (map 51 S.W.) arriving at 1:45 a.m.

This is an interesting area, just like Astcote; a farming hamlet with single story red brick houses with red tiled roofs, well, what's left of them. It must be about the same size as Astcote and, just like Astcote, we entered from a ridge down a narrow lane. The only difference between Astcote and here is that here, the houses are in ruin, the fields are full of trenches, there are few trees and the sounds of birds singing and dogs barking is replaced by deathly quiet with the occasional bomb exploding. I bet, in another time, this place would look and sound wonderful.

3:45   Zero hour at 3:45 am

The Battalion was not engaged in the first part of the operations.

Bit lucky there being in reserve.

After retirement of positions W of CHÉRISY and FONTAINE-CROISILLE the Battalion was ordered to counter attack and occupy FONTAINE TRENCH from O.32.a.5.3 to O.26.C.2.0 and the circular trench in rear of it.

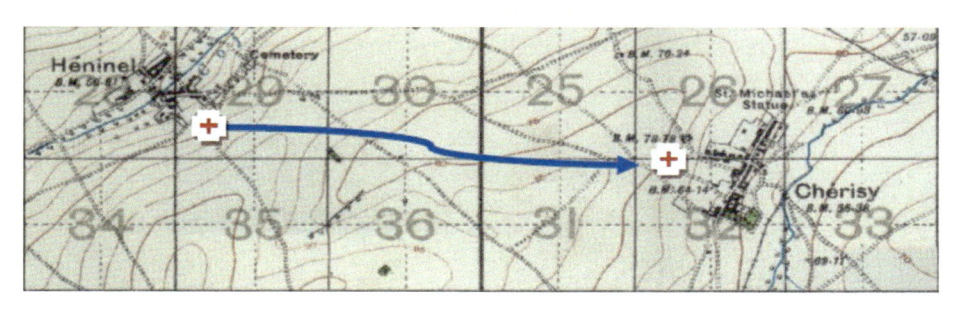

Orders had been received that the bombardment was to start at 5-30 p.m. for half an hour, then a pause for a quarter of an hour and the rolling barrage would open at 6-15 p.m. 200 yards in front of our trench, but this was later postponed for one hour.

Battalion was in position at 5-30 p.m. (all in front line trench) with the LEICESTERSHIRE REGIMENT (110 Infantry Brigade) on the right and the 7th QUEENS (55th Brigade) on the left. These Battalions were to attack simultaneously after a preliminary bombardment as stated. The rolling barrage opened and the Battalion attacked with 2 Companies. 2 platoons in the front line and 2 platoons 2nd line. A and D Companies were in support. Of the attacking Companies, B Company under Captain Mobbs were on the right and C Company under Captain Shepherd on the left. A Company were on the right, D Company on the left as supporting Companies.

D Company furnished a bombing party (1 NCO and 8 men) who advanced down CABLE TRENCH with the leading wave of the assaulting Company. They also furnished carrying parties for bombs and SAA for C Company, down CABLE TRENCH running towards CHÉRISY from O.31.b.4.9.

Madness, shear madness! Walking in file behind a barrage where some of the shells are falling short - shear madness. Crack, crack, crack, thud, thud, thud... Christ, that thud was close; he's a goner...slow down Bob, don't be so hasty...

Captain Mobbs is shouting for us to keep in line and file and urging us on...he's as mad as we are but there's no alternative...

B and C Companies advanced as close to the barrage as possible having several casualties from the barrage.

My bubble's burst... it's quiet... no ringing in my ears... I'm not moving... they are... I can't feel anything... God, what's happening... I'm scared...

I'm NO LONGER WITH MY BODY

The hostile Machine Gun fire which swept the area they had to cross was as bad as in the attack of the morning. B Company (right assaulting Company) having 50% casualties by the time they reached within 50 yards of the enemy wire – having covered nearly 900 yards. They found the wire intact, the bombardment not having touched it, and the machine gun fire from the right flank as well as from the front rendered further advance impossible.

So we didn't win that one. Looking at the "walk into the storm" tactics, they didn't work on the 1st July 1916 so why did they think it would work now? If we'd have used our "small blobs at irregular intervals and at our own speed" tactics that Colonel Ripley endorsed to such great effect, I may have survived the battle and, probably the war.

RESTING WITH MY MATES

I heard them say that Unit Number 22554 engraved on the spoon identified the mangled mess as Private Robert Furness, me. They recorded the details and buried what was left of me where I fell, just outside Chérisy, at map reference 51b.O.32.a.40.50. The cross on the map below marks the spot and it's called Rue des Agaches. It's on the slope overlooking Chérisy and, I suppose it's ironic really, it's a stone's throw from the Hamlet's cemetery.

Chérisy sits down behind a row of mangled trees and you can see for miles from where I'm buried.

Thinking back on my first comments about the pleasing views available through open fields around Saisseval, little did I imagine at the time that these same open fields would be a major factor in my death.

It's quite ironic really when I think of it, I started life in Astcote and during the first 33 years of my life I travelled about 28 miles to become a boot maker. In the next 18 months I had no real choice but to travel about 1500 miles to die as a trained killer, in a foreign hamlet just like Astcote.

FINAL JOURNEY

Just after the 11th anniversary of my passing.

16th May 1928

The cross, at map reference 51b.A.16.b.85.40, marks where I am finally resting with my mates. It's in the Commune of Roclincourt's Arras Road Cemetery, Plot 3, Row K, Grave No. 5 but my headstone has still not been erected.

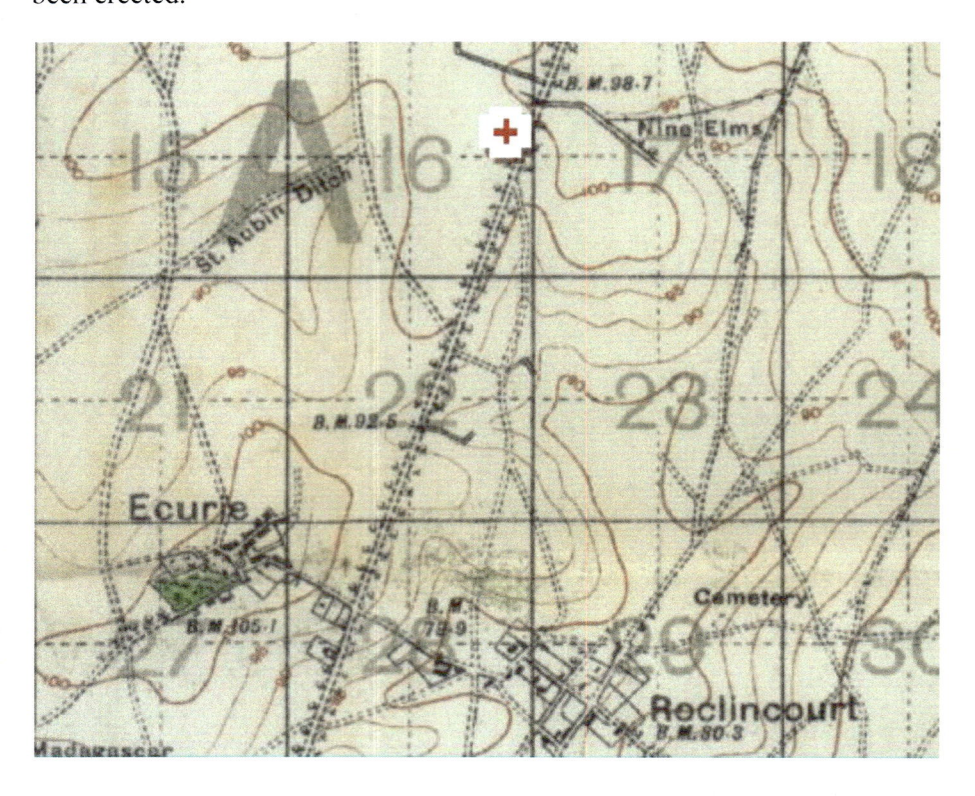

20th May 1928

Four days later, Army Form W 3872, Final Grave Registration Report No. 4 Schedule No. 41c, indicates my headstone has been erected and my final resting place is now secure in this corner of a foreign field that is forever Irchester. You'll notice that they have me down as being 36 when I was, in fact, only 35.

THE CONNECTION

But that isn't the end of my story…

My grandson, David Smart, had been trying to discover the whereabouts of my medals and Memorial Plaque (War Penny or Dead Man's Penny) for a long time and Ken, during the research period, had also been surfing the internet with the same quest but nothing was found.

Medals were not on Ken's mind when, on the 3rd May 2017, after a leisurely breakfast, he and his siblings went to the Thiepval Memorial to buy two wreaths and then onto Chérisy where I was killed. After a relaxed wander up and down Cable Trench and soaking up the atmosphere with some of the bombs that rained down on us, they drove to my grave in the Arras Road Cemetery.

About 200 yards from the cemetery Ken pulled over to let a car through from the narrow section of the approach road and the occupants of both cars waved at each other to acknowledge the respectful gestures; the United Kingdom car number plate was half mentioned in conversation.

On arrival, to everybody's utter surprise, a wreath was already laying on my grave. The Cemetery Guest Book indicated a S Gooch had been the only other visitor but there was no other contact details apart from, Brightling, E. Sussex. As it was pouring down with rain they paid their respects, took a few photographs and went onto the Vimy Ridge Memorial.

The sun was shining on their return from Vimy so they agreed to drop in for some more photos around my grave and it was here that my great grandson Kevin took a closer look at the wreath note and found Stuart's email address on the back.

The following emails were sent and received that evening:

On 3 May 2017 16:53, Ken Brawn <ksbrawn@yahoo.co.uk> wrote:
Hi Stuart,

I see you were at Robert's grave today and I think we (in the black Nissan) pulled over to let you out of the cemetery road. Please see the photo's attached.

My names Ken and Robert is my Great Grandfather.

From let to right on the photo, there is my brother Kevin, sister Anita, me and my older brother Tony.

We are staying at Avril's Guesthouse Avril Williams Guesthouse and Tearooms until Friday morning.

It would be good to get in touch because I have just finished a book on Robert and the photos of today are the last I need for the book.

Looking forward to hearing from you,
Ken Brawn
+447955120194

Subject: Re: Robert Furness

From: Stuart Gooch (stuartgooch@yahoo.co.uk)

To: ksbrawn@yahoo.co.uk;

Date: Wednesday, 3 May 2017, 19:24

Hello family,
What can you say, to actually past by each other.
I've just spoken to Mum who says you are Mary's children.Is that right ?
You say you have written a book!
Hold the front page. I have his two service medals and
the death penny.
Also the only personal item to be sent back,which was a knife,fork and spoon set in a pouch. Apparently arriving a year to the day he died.
Unfortunately I am back home in Sussex , are you heading home on Friday and what route are you taking?

My mum is Iris Gooch nee Furness her dad was Bob Furness the only surviving son.
I think your mum and mine were first cousins.
I've only got a dodgy mobile at the moment but mum's
Phone no. Is XXXXXXXXXXX and she lives in Eastbourne.
It would be great to catch you on the way home even if it's a service station.
But we will meet.
Stuart

Needless to say, Ken and his siblings were quite emotional at the news of the medals and this meeting is a fitting end to Ken's quest to document my life.

It's also interesting to see the parallels between Ken's and my life:

26th September 2015 – Birthday message from Sharon to Ken and Ancestry link discussion
5th October 2015 – Sharon sends Ancestry link to Ken and he "discovers" me
8th October 1915 – I hear about conscription
19th November 1915 – I join the 6th Northants to go to war in France
20th November 2015 – Out of the blue, Ken gets an offer of work in France
26th September 1916 – I was fighting in the Brawn Trench at Thiepval
26th September 1952 – Ken was born 35 years after my death at the age of 35
3rd May 1917 – I was killed
3rd May 1918 – My medals, Memorial Plaque and my knife, fork and spoon, were received by my loving Trudy.
3rd May 2017 – Ken, through the email above, found the missing medals and my personal effects.
Thanks to my daughter Lily's inner sense, Ken's mother lived to tell the ironic story of my daughter Phyllis May's death which allowed Ken to be born to tell this story

AT PEACE

So there you have it. You now know about my life, where I travelled, what I did, where I was killed and where I'm buried. The questions of why I did it and how I was killed can be answered in that I had no choice but to volunteer to give my family pride in me and if you haven't pieced it together, I was blown to pieces by our own shrapnel shells.

Lying here in my little Arras plot, surrounded by my mates and descendants exactly 100 years later, I can now fully let go of the heavy burden of what would happen to my family if I was killed.

I can now smile in the knowledge that my short life with my loving Trudy and children has borne good fruit and our descendants live a happy life in relative peace and prosperity.

My sacrifice during those months of war has given my descendants the freedom of what would have been my tomorrow and through my reconnected family, medals and life story

I AM
ALIVE
AGAIN

THANK YOU

IN MY FOOTSTEPS
5th to 8th May 2016

THE BATTLE OF ALBERT
1st July 1916 (2016)

Black Alley looking towards Pomiers Redoubt

Pomiers Redoubt looking towards Black Alley

THE BATTLE OF TRONES WOOD
14th July 1916 (2016)

18th Division Memorial

100 Years to the hour later - 3:30p.m.
Position we held having captured Trones Wood

THE BATTLE OF THIEPVAL RIDGE
26th September 1916 (2016)

100 Years to the minute later – 9:15a.m.
Where we formed up prior to the Thiepval attack

18th Division, 54th Inf. Brig. 6th Northampton Memorial – 3:30pm

NORTH WEST OF CHÉRISY
3rd May 1917 (2017)

Where I was killed

Still Being Dug Up

Cable Trench

A CORNER OF A FOREIGN FIELD THAT IS, FOREVER, IRCHESTER
Brawn, Smart and Gooch Wreaths

OTHER RELEVANT PHOTOS

On The Brawn Trench

David and Andrew Smart

CONCENTRATION OF GRAVES - BURIAL RETURNS DOCUMENT

From the left, column 4 identifies exactly where I was found to within a few square feet.

Colum 6 & 7 show that I was "identified" by clothing and equipment and my number on the spoon – obviously, there wasn't much left of me to identify.

The War Diary records, *"B and C Companies advanced as close to the barrage as possible having several casualties..."* and *"B Company ... having 50% casualties by the time they reached within 50 yards of the enemy wire.... They found the wire intact, the bombardment not having touched it..."* Taking the totality of the above into consideration, Ken has concluded that shrapnel shells were used and if I'd have been killed by machine guns before the enemy wire, there would have been more of me to identify...

None of us will know the real end but this being the end of my story, I think we can accept this as a fitting conclusion.

KEN, IN REFLECTION

Sitting at my dad's kitchen table, I was surfing the internet and my troubled personal circumstances. I wasn't absorbing what the internet was delivering because I was vividly aware that my marriage was experiencing major difficulties, I'd spent the past few months with my dad during the discovery and treatment of his cancer, there was little chance of future work because retirement was less than two years away and I was in no doubt whatsoever that I had absolutely no idea what tomorrow would bring.

It was the 5th October 2015 and the laptop beep moved my thoughts back to the screen. Sharon Brawn had kindly sent the link to her research into our family trees so that my dad and I could see the results of her efforts. I could never have prophesied, in my wildest dreams, what I was to experience through the consequences of the single click on that link and the workings of "fate".

As we viewed the data, Robert's entry hit me between the eyes – here was the man I had heard about and this was the moment where time and circumstance melded together so that I could put substance to the long held thought of, "Who was this person who had fought in World War One?"

My curiosity piqued, I gladly probed deeper and deeper and entered a wonderful world of exploration of intertwined family and world history which would allow me, exactly 100 years later to the minute, to mentally replay and physically walk in my great grandfather's footsteps and incredibly, experience the last minutes of his life.

There are times in my life when I have been in awe at the situation presenting itself; sitting in my pushchair wondering what was behind the white house on the horizon, my first unaccompanied train journey as a 16 year old, the birth of my children, poking my head through the submarine hatch to view every new port of call, the freezing monochrome world of the North Pole during its 6 months of darkness, consuming champagne and caviar while flying faster than a bullet in Concorde, looking up at Table Mountain on a sun kissed day, unaccompanied lunch in the Chernobyl Nuclear Power Station canteen, the crunch of minus 35°C snow in Ukraine, touching the remains of the radio shack my brother

Kevin built on an isolated beach during the Falkland's War, pristine Antarctica, kicking the junk mail to one side at the end of my Arctic / Antarctica / Arctic adventure and, on my 64th birthday, hearing great grandfather Robert's name and exploits being read out while standing on top of the BRAWN trench at the Thiepval Memorial as I was transported back 100 years to the very same minute of the very same day to experience the heat of battle for the very ground on which I stood.

The word, awesome, doesn't readily describe the visual and mental vistas of the contrasting eras of war and peace. One minute I was alone in a peaceful and technicolored tended landscape, next, I was with Great Grandfather in the heat of battle, fighting for his life in a devastated monochrome terrain and next, I was experiencing the superimposed eras – a truly amazing experience, that I am reliving as I'm writing this. I can state openly, this single experience has enriched my life beyond words.

FATE?

I believe I can reasonably control my future by defining its parameters and then working to achieve them. "Reasonably" is the key word because there are external influences that can't be foreseen and hence, factored in. External factors, can be split into two, the explained and "the weird", or, as it's sometimes labelled, fate.

Leaving the explained to one side and shaking my head from side to side in wonderment, I have this weird feeling that I wasn't supposed to find Great Grandfather until the time was right.

You may say I'm being a bit melodramatic but in reflection, I have to ask the question of why, when the time was never right before, out of the blue, I should receive my ancestry history and get the same offer of work that I'd turned down twice in the preceding 5 years? These two events triggered further events that allowed me to follow and actually walk Great Grandfather's wartime journey 100 years, to the minute, later.

Looking a bit deeper, why should my father fully recover from cancer and another totally unconnected person decide to leave his job at the same time as, 100 years earlier, Great Grandfather finally decided to volunteer to join the Army?

Why, as you will read later, did Nan Smart tell my mum not to stay with Aunt Phyllis on the night she was killed by German bombs in World War Two and why was I the only child that Grandfather Smart wanted to join the Army? Why was I born, 35 years to the day after Great Grandfather (who was 35 when he died) had fought and helped capture the ground that contained the BRAWN trench and which was destined to become the British and South African site of the Somme Memorial. Also, why was I born English but adopted South African Citizenship?

Why had I known for decades about, "the ancestor in the Great War" but life's jigsaw had never come together for me to delve deeper? Why did everything come together on my 63rd birthday? Fate?

I've had a very productive and wonderful life where I've been able to greatly enrich other people's lives and with the birth of my 4th grandchild, I hope I will enrich their lives through this book which covers one of my greatest experiences, the discovery of the truly remarkable life of great grandfather Robert Furness.

We always think life is hard but when compared to Great Grandfather's short life and the problems and the decisions he had to make, our lives are incredibly easy and comfortable.

I will leave this thought for my descendents; I believe that if you keep the magnitude of your problems and decisions in perspective with those Great Grandfather had to make, I believe your futures will be far more productive, joyful and rewarding. Stay chilled…

THE END

OTHER FAMILY MEMBERS RECOGNISED

1914-15 Star

Known as "Pip", it is a bronze medal authorized in 1918. It was awarded to all who served in any theatre of war against Germany between 5th August 1914 and 31st December 1915. The recipient had to have received the British War Medal and the Victory Medal

BRITISH WAR MEDAL

Known as "Squeak", it was instituted on 26 July 1919 for award to those who had rendered service between 5 August 1914, the day following the British declaration of war against the German Empire, and the armistice of 11 November 1918

VICTORY MEDAL

Known as "Wilfred", it is a World War One campaign medal of Britain and her then colonies and dominions (e.g. Canada, Australia, New Zealand). The medal was issued to most of those who were awarded the British War Medal - it was never awarded singly.

SERGEANT WILLIAM ALFRED SMART
AUTHOR'S MATERNAL GREAT GRANDFATHER

Born 29th May 1875 in 18 Well Street, Wellingborough
Died 10th March 1940 in 16 Waterloo Buildings, Wellingborough

7th Northamptonshire Regiment	No. 15929
Royal Fusiliers	No. 103540
Labour Corps	No. 408236
Lancashire Fusiliers	No. 49992

MEDALS AWARDED

1914-15 STAR
BRITISH WAR MEDAL
VICTORY MEDAL

LANCE CORPORAL WILLIAM EDWIN JOHN SMART
AUTHOR'S MATERNAL GREAT UNCLE

Birth APRIL 1896 • Wellingborough, Northamptonshire
Death MAR 1946 • Wellingborough, Northamptonshire

Northamptonshire Regiment	No. 38335
Labour Corps	No. 89749

MEDALS AWARDED

BRITISH WAR MEDAL
VICTORY MEDAL

PRIVATE TOM MacDONALD SMART
AUTHOR'S MATERNAL GRANDFATHER

Birth 6th MAY 1900 • Wellingborough, Northamptonshire
Death 30th MARCH 1970 • Irchester, Northamptonshire

We know very little about Grampy Tom Smart's contribution apart from that he was part of the Occupying Forces after the end of World War One and he was also a member of the Home Guard during World War Two.

To Grampy Smart's request and delight, I was given the middle name of Stanley after Grampy Smart's hero, Sir Stanley Matthews, CBE. Grampy Smart had hoped that I would be a footballer in the Army and I am very grateful that Grampy Smart didn't show any dissatisfaction when I became a rugby player in the Royal Navy. ☺

INNOCENT FAMILY VICTIMS OF WORLD WAR TWO

On the 19th May 1941, my mother Mary had arranged to go and stay with her aunt, Phyllis May White (née Furness) and at the very last minute my grandmother, Lily Smart (née Furness), said she couldn't go. When my mother asked why, her mother replied, "I just have a funny feeling and I don't want you to go."

In the early hours of the next day, a stray German Bomber dropped 4 bombs on Irchester, two landing in Farndish Road. Only one exploded, at the junction with East Street and directly in front of number twenty. The bomb fractured a gas main and it was concluded that six adults and three children, including my mother's aunt Phyllis and cousin Colin, were not killed directly by the blast but succumbed to the effects of gas whilst trapped under the rubble.

They are all buried in Irchester cemetery and at the 50th anniversary in 1991, a plaque was placed on the village war memorial.

Thanks to that sense, that none of us can explain, my mother lived to tell the story and I was born to tell this story.

It's ironic that Phyllis shared the same 8th July birth date with Robert; he was killed by the Germans in May of World War One and she was killed by them in May of World War Two

PHYLLIS MAY WHITE (née FURNESS)
AUTHOR'S MATERNAL GREAT AUNT

Birth 8th JULY 1914 • 6 Fish's Terrace, Irchester, Northamptonshire
Death 20th MAY 1941 • 20 Farndish Road, Irchester, Northamptonshire

COLIN EDWARD JAMES WHITE
AUTHOR'S MATERNAL FIRST COUSIN ONCE REMOVED

Birth 11th JAN 1937 • 188 Priory Road, Wellingborough, Northamptonshire
Death 20th MAY 1941 • 20 Farndish Road Irchester, Northamptonshire

ABOUT THE AUTHOR

Great Grandson of Robert Furness
(8.7.1881 to 3.5.1917) Astcote, Northants
and Gertrude Frances Furness (née Stokes)
(1879 to 1930) Rushden, Northants.

Grandson of Robert's daughter
Lily Smart (née Furness)
(29.3.1908 to 17.8.1963)
13 Greens Yard, Rushden, Northants.
Married Tom Smart.

Son of Robert's granddaughter
Francis Mary Brawn (née Smart)
(always known as Mary)
(14.3.1929 to 29.4.2011)
School Hill, Irchester, Northants
Married Bert Brawn.

AUTHOR'S FURNESS FAMILY TREE

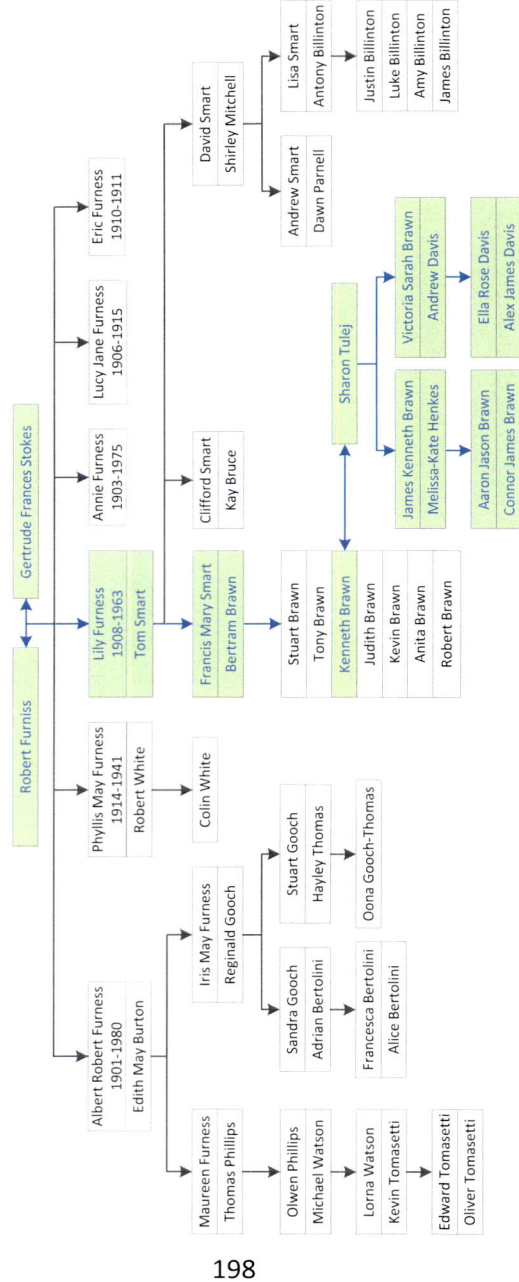

- Robert Furniss — Gertrude Frances Stokes
  - Albert Robert Furness 1901-1980 — Edith May Burton
    - Maureen Furness — Thomas Phillips
      - Olwen Phillips — Michael Watson
        - Lorna Watson — Kevin Tomasetti
          - Edward Tomasetti
          - Oliver Tomasetti
    - Iris May Furness — Reginald Gooch
      - Sandra Gooch — Adrian Bertolini
        - Francesca Bertolini
        - Alice Bertolini
      - Stuart Gooch — Hayley Thomas
        - Oona Gooch-Thomas
    - Phyllis May Furness 1914-1941 — Robert White
      - Colin White
  - **Lily Furness 1908-1963 — Tom Smart**
    - **Francis Mary Smart — Bertram Brawn**
      - Stuart Brawn
      - Tony Brawn
      - **Kenneth Brawn — Sharon Tulej**
        - **James Kenneth Brawn — Melissa-Kate Henkes**
          - **Aaron Jason Brawn**
          - **Connor James Brawn**
        - **Victoria Sarah Brawn — Andrew Davis**
          - **Ella Rose Davis**
          - **Alex James Davis**
      - Judith Brawn
      - Kevin Brawn
      - Anita Brawn
      - Robert Brawn
    - Clifford Smart — Kay Bruce
  - Annie Furness 1903-1975
    - David Smart — Shirley Mitchell
      - Lisa Smart — Antony Billinton
        - Justin Billinton
        - Luke Billinton
        - Amy Billinton
        - James Billinton
      - Andrew Smart — Dawn Parnell
  - Lucy Jane Furness 1906-1915
  - Eric Furness 1910-1911

198

Robert's association with the military has descended through the generations, without break, to Ken who, during his days in the Royal Navy submarine service, was directly involved in the Cold and Falkland Wars and the Irish Republican Army Troubles.

Bert Brawn, Ken's father, served in the Royal Navy at the end of World War Two clearing sea mines in various locations but specifically in the Mediterranean and Red Sea.

Ken's Uncle, John Brawn, saw action in the Royal Navy during World War Two in Africa, the Middle and Far East.

Kevin, Ken's brother, was a Royal Marine who participated in two Gulf Wars, the Bosnian and Falkland Wars and 4 Tours of duty in Northern Ireland.

Sister Anita served in the Women's Royal Navy Service where she met her husband Robert Carter, who served with the Fleet Air Arm in the Bosnian and Afghanistan Wars and also with NATO in Europe.

The above have their own stories to tell, some harrowing with medals won but the direct association with the military stopped at Ken's children who, thankfully, live a full life of relative peace.

SACRIFICE FOR THE GREATER GOOD
IS A PRICE WE SOMETIMES HAVE TO PAY
BUT THE GREATER GOOD
MUST BE EXPLICITLY
DEFINED, QUANTIFIED AND AGREED
BEFORE
THE DECISION TO SACRIFICE IS MADE

Kenneth S Brawn 2015

THE SOLDIER
by Rupert Brooke (1887-1915)

If I should die, think only this of me:
    That there's some corner of a foreign field
That is forever England. There shall be
    In that rich earth a richer dust concealed;
A dust whom England bore, shaped, made aware,
    Gave, once, her flowers to love, her ways to roam,
A body of England's, breathing English air,
    Washed by the rivers, blest by suns of home.

And think, this heart, all evil shed away,
    A pulse in the Eternal mind, no less
        Gives somewhere back the thoughts by England given,
Her sights and sounds; dreams happy as her day;
    And laughter, learnt of friends; and gentleness,
        In hearts at peace, under an English heaven.
(1914)

IN FLANDERS FIELD
John McCrae (1872-1918)

In Flanders fields the poppies blow
Between the crosses, row on row,
That mark our place; and in the sky
The larks, still bravely singing, fly
Scarce heard amid the guns below.

We are the Dead. Short days ago
We lived, felt dawn, saw sunset glow,
Loved and were loved, and now we lie
In Flanders fields.

Take up our quarrel with the foe:
To you from failing hands we throw
The torch; be yours to hold it high.
If ye break faith with us who die
We shall not sleep, though poppies grow
In Flanders fields.

HISTORY OF THE POPPY EMBLEM

Extract of
Inspiration for the Flanders Fields Memorial Poppy, and
Anna Guérin: "The French Poppy Lady"
From the Great War 1914 – 1918 website
http://www.greatwar.co.uk/article/remembrance-poppy.htm

There can be a bit of a controversy on who came up with the idea first and I leave the reader to decide. The following is extracted, with kind thanks, from the Great War 1914 – 1918 website.

Firstly - **Anna Guérin** (photo courtesy of Heather Johnson)

A French woman by the name of Madame Anna E Guérin was a representative of the French YMCA Secretariat and she considered that artificial poppies could be made and sold as a way of raising money for the benefit of the French people, especially the orphaned children, who were suffering as a result of the war.

She was the founder of the "American and French Children's League" through which she organized French women, children and war veterans to make artificial poppies out of cloth.

Her intention was that these poppies would be sold and the proceeds could be used to help fund the restoration of the war-torn regions of France.

Anna was determined to introduce the idea of the memorial poppy to the nations which had been Allied with France during the First World War. During 1921 she made visits or sent representatives to America, Australia, Britain, Canada and New Zealand.

Life and Work of Anna Guérin

A lovely website, poppyladymadameguerin.wordpress.com, researched and released by Heather Johnson in November 2015, is devoted to Anna and her work with the poppy and Remembrance.

Spreading the Message of the Memorial Poppy

1921: French Poppies Sold in America

In 1921 Madame Guérin made arrangements for the first nationwide distribution across America of poppies made in France by the American and French Childrens' League.

The funds raised from this venture went directly to the League to help with rehabilitation and resettlement of the areas of France devastated by the First World War. Millions of these French-made artificial poppies were sold in America between 1920 and 1924.

5 July 1921: Canada adopts the Flower of Remembrance

Madame Anna Guérin travelled to Canada, where she met with representatives of the Great War Veterans Association of Canada. This organization later became the Royal Canadian Legion. The Great War Veterans Association adopted the poppy as its national flower of Remembrance on 5 July 1921.

11 November 1921: The First British Legion Poppy Day Appeal

In 1921 Anna Guérin sent some French women to London to sell their artificial red poppies. This was the first introduction to the British people of Moina Michael's (see below) idea of the Memorial Poppy.

Madame Guérin went in person to visit Field Marshal Earl Douglas Haig, founder and President of The British Legion. She persuaded him to adopt the Flanders Poppy as an emblem for The Legion. This was formalized in the autumn of 1921.

The first British Poppy Day Appeal was launched that year, in the run up to 11 November 1921. It was the third anniversary of the Armistice to end the Great

War. Proceeds from the sale of artificial French-made poppies were given to ex-servicemen in need of welfare and financial support.

Since that time the red poppy has been sold each year by The British Legion from mid October to raise funds in support of the organization's charitable work.

May 1922: French-made Poppies Sold in the United States

In 1922 the organization of the American and French Childrens' League was disbanded. Madam Guérin was still keen to raise funds for the French people who had suffered the destruction of their communities. She asked the American organization called Veterans of Foreign Wars (VFW) to help her with the distribution of her French-made poppies throughout the United States.

That year the VFW assisted with the sale of the poppies in America to help keep up the much needed funds for the battle-scarred areas of France. The poppies were sold before Memorial Day which was observed at that time on 30th May. This was the first time that a United States war veterans' organization took on the task of selling the red poppy as a symbol of Remembrance and as a means of fund raising. The VFW decided to adopt the poppy as its own official memorial flower.

1923: The American Legion Sells Poppies in the United States

In 1923 the American Legion sold poppies in the United States which were made by a French company.

Secondly - Miss Moina Belle Michael "The Poppy Lady"

The origin of the red Flanders poppy as a modern-day symbol of Remembrance was the inspiration of an American, Miss Moina Belle Michael "The Poppy Lady"

It was on Saturday morning, 9 November 1918, two days before the Armistice was declared at 11 o'clock on 11 November and Moina was on duty at the YMCA Overseas War Secretaries' headquarters in New York.

Leafing through the latest November edition of the

"Ladies Home Journal" she came across a vivid colour illustration with the poem entitled "We Shall Not Sleep". This was an alternative name sometimes used for John McCrae's poem, which was also called "In Flanders Fields". Lieutenant-Colonel John McCrae had died of pneumonia several months earlier on 28 January 1918.

Moina had come across the poem before, but reading it on this occasion she found herself transfixed by the last verse:

> Take up our quarrel with the foe:
> To you from failing hands we throw
> The torch; be yours to hold it high.
> If ye break faith with us who die
> We shall not sleep, though poppies grow
> In Flanders fields.

In her autobiography, entitled "The Miracle Flower", Moina describes this experience as deeply spiritual. She felt as though she was actually being called in person by the voices which had been silenced by death.

At that moment Moina made a personal pledge to "keep the faith". She vowed always to wear a red poppy of Flanders Fields as a sign of remembrance. It would become an emblem for "keeping the faith with all who died".
Compelled to make a note of this pledge she scribbled down a response on the back of a used envelope. She titled her poem "We Shall Keep the Faith".

The first verse read like this:

> Oh! you who sleep in Flanders Fields,
> Sleep sweet - to rise anew!
> We caught the torch you threw
> And holding high, we keep the Faith
> With All who died.

Three men attending the conference arrived at Moina's desk and, on behalf of the delegates, they asked her to accept a cheque for 10 dollars in appreciation of the effort she had made, at her own expense, to brighten up the place with flowers.

She was touched by the gesture and replied that she would buy twenty-five red poppies with the money. She showed them the Ladies Home Journal illustration for John McCrae's poem "In Flanders Fields" together with her response "We Shall Keep the Faith". The delegates took both poems back into the Conference.

After searching the shops for some time that day Moina found one large and twenty-four small artificial red silk poppies in Wanamaker's department store. When she returned to duty at the YMCA Headquarters later that evening the delegates from the Conference crowded round her asking for poppies to wear.

Keeping one poppy for her coat collar she gave out the rest of the poppies to the enthusiastic delegates. According to Moina, this was the first group-effort asking for poppies to wear in memory of "all who died in Flanders Fields". Since this group had given her the money with which she had bought them, she considered that she had made the first sale of the Flanders Fields Memorial Poppy on 9 November 1918.

Moina, through letters to the press, was determined to get the Poppy emblem adopted as a United States national memorial symbol and she was encouraged by the positive reaction to the idea.

Moira realized that, after the war, the numerous signs related to the war, the Red Cross, War Loan insignia, Service Flags, etc., which had been evident all over the United States during its involvement in the war, would gradually be removed. She considered that a replacement emblem, the red poppy, could be used to fill those empty spaces as a symbolic reminder of those who had not returned home to celebrate the end of the war.

Her religious upbringing inspired her to believe that the Flanders Memorial Poppy was indeed a spiritual symbol with more meaning behind it than pure sentimentalism. She likened the new optimism of a world returned to peace after the "war to end all wars" to the magnificent rainbow which appeared in the sky after the terrible flood in the bible.

She began a tireless campaign, at her own expense, starting with a letter to her congressman in December 1918. In the letter she asked him to put the idea to the War Department, which he immediately did.

She decided to act swiftly so that this new national emblem would be available as pins, on postcards, etc. in time for the signing of the peace treaty at Versailles in June 1919.

Originally Moina intended to use the simple red, four petal field poppy of Flanders as the Memorial Poppy emblem and she was put in touch with the designer, Mr Lee Keedick, who offered to design the national emblem.

In December 1918 he produced the final design, which was accepted. This emblem consisted of a border of blue on a white background with the Torch of Liberty and a Poppy entwined in the centre, containing the colours of the Allied flags: red, white, blue, black, green and yellow. The design appealed to Moina.

The "Torch and Poppy" emblem was first used officially on 14 February 1919 in Carnegie Hall, New York City. The event was a lecture given by the Canadian ace pilot, Colonel William Avery "Billy" Bishop, VC, CB, DSO & Bar, MC DFC, ED. His lecture was titled "Air Fighting in Flanders Fields". As the lecture ended a large flag with the new torch and poppy emblem on it was unfurled at the back of the stage.

However, in spite of the interest raised by the appearance of the new emblem at the time, and Moina's continued efforts to publicize the campaign, this emblem was not taken up by any group or individual to help establish it as a national symbol.

There was so little public interest in the enterprise that eventually the emblem's designer, Mr Keedick, abandoned his interest in pursuing Moina's campaign.

Moina was beginning to lose hope that the Memorial Poppy idea would ever come to fruition. However, in the early 1920s a number of organizations did adopt the red poppy as a result of Moina's dedicated campaign.

In August 1920 Moina discovered, by chance, that the Georgia Department of the American Legion was to convene on the 20th of that month in Atlanta. Prior to the convention she searched out the delegates and the Navy representative promised to present her case for the Memorial Poppy to the convention.

The Georgia Convention subsequently adopted the Memorial Poppy but omitted the Torch symbol. The Convention also agreed to endorse the movement to have the Poppy adopted by the National American Legion and resolved to urge each member of the American Legion in Georgia to wear a red poppy annually on 11 November.

One month later, on 29 September 1920, the National American Legion convened in Cleveland. The Convention agreed on the use of the Flanders Fields Memorial Poppy as the United States' national emblem of Remembrance.

ORIGINS OF THE TWO MINUTES PAUSE

The above image, taken in 1942, is rare and unique. It shows a South African serviceman and Capetonian's standing to attention for two minutes silence signalled by the firing of the Signal Hill noon day gun.

So how did this unique practice become a worldwide standard for remembrance?

Funnily, it all started in Cape Town and South Africans can stand proud of what they have given the world when, on Remembrance Sunday and 11th November Armistice day, the western world, in remembrance, stands silent for two minutes.

The end of World War 1 – Armistice Day

At 05.30 in the morning of 11th November 1918, in a remote railway siding in the heart of the forest of Compiègne in northern France, the French, British and Germans signed the Armistice of Compiègne in French Marshal and Supreme Commander of the Allied Armies, Ferdinand Foch's railway carriage.

Soon, wires were humming with the message, "Hostilities will cease at 11.00 today November 11th. Troops will stand fast on the line reached at that hour…". Thus, at 11.00 a.m. on the 11th November 1918 (French time) the guns fell silent after more than four years of continuous warfare that had witnessed the most horrific casualties and carnage. World War One (then known as the Great War) had ended.

The time and date attained an important significance in post war years and it became universally associated with remembering those that died in World War One and subsequent wars and conflicts. The Two Minutes silence became the universal expression of remembrance to all who paid the supreme sacrifice… and it all began in Cape Town, South Africa.

Cape Town's unique remembrance during World War One

When the first casualty lists, recording the horrific loss of life in the Battle of the Somme in 1916, were announced in Cape Town, Mr. JA Eagar, a Cape Town businessman, suggested to his church that the congregation observe a special silent pause to remember those in the South African casualty list. It was also the church that Sir Percy Fitzpatrick, the famous South African author of "Jock of the Bushveld" attended.

In May 1918, from a suggestion by Councillor Mr. RR Brydon, the Mayor of Cape Town, Councillor H Hands (later Sir Harry Hands), in a letter to the Cape Times, initiated a period of silence to remember the events unfolding on the battlefields of Europe and the sacrifices being made. Mr. Brydon's son, Maj. Walter Brydon was killed on 12th April 1918 after surviving being wounded three times and gassed once.

For the first time, on 14th May 1918, a silent three minute pause followed the firing of the Signal Hill Noon Gun, the most audible signal with which to coordinate the event across the city of Cape Town. Everything and everyone stopped and bowed their heads in silent prayer for those in the trenches in Flanders.

As soon as the city fell silent, a trumpeter on the balcony of the Fletcher and Cartwright's Building on the corner of Adderley and Darling Streets sounded the Last Post, the melancholy strains of which reverberated through the city. Reveille was played at the end of the midday pause.

Newspaper articles described how trams, taxis and private vehicles stopped, pedestrians came to a halt and most men bared their heads. People stopped what they were doing at their places of work and sat or stood silently. The result of the Mayor's appeal exceeded all expectations. One journalist described a young woman, dressed in black, who came to a halt on the pavement and furtively dabbed at her eyes with a handkerchief. "One could not but wonder what personal interest she had in the act of remembrance", he wrote.

A few days later Sir Harry, whose son, Capt. Richard Hands, who had been a member of "Brydon's Battery" and had been mortally wounded in the same battle in which Maj. Brydon had been killed, decided to shorten the duration of the pause to two minutes, "in order to better retain its hold on the people".

In terms of the meaning of "two minutes" it was also argued that the first minute is for thanksgiving for those that survived and the second is to remember the fallen.

The midday pause continued daily in Cape Town until the 17th January 1919 but was later revived in Cape Town during the Second World War. It had, however, become a pause throughout the British Commonwealth from the 11th November 1919.

Step in Sir Percy Fitzpatrick

Sir Percy, after the horrific loss of life at Delville Wood had became known and the casualty lists had been read out, was impressed by the period of silence kept in his local church. He had a personal interest in the daily remembrance as his son, Maj. Nugent Fitzpatrick, battery commander of 71st Siege Battery, was killed on the 14th December 1917 by a chance shell fired at long range.

Sir Percy was understandably deeply affected by the loss of his favourite son and was also so moved by the dignity and effectiveness of the two minute pause in Cape Town that the date and time of the Armistice inspired him to an annual commemoration on an Imperial basis.

The King Decrees

Sir Percy wrote to The Rt. Hon The Viscount Milner GCB GCMG PC describing the silence that fell on the city during this daily ritual and, taking into consideration that the guns of war finally fell silent at 11:00 on the 11th day of the 11th month (November), Sir Percy felt that the idea of observing the two-minute silence at that time and on that date would give the Act of Homage greater impact; he then proposed that this become an official part of the annual service on Armistice Day.

The meaning behind Sir Percy's proposal was stated as:
It is due to the women, who have lost and suffered and borne so much, with whom the thought is ever present.
It is due to the children that they know to whom they owe their dear fought freedom.
It is due to the men, and from them, as men.
But far and away, above all else, it is due to those who gave their all, sought no recompense, and with whom we can never re-pay – our Glorious and Immortal Dead.

Sir Percy's letter was received by Viscount Milner on the 4th November 1919, reviewed and accepted by the War Cabinet on November 5th and was immediately approved by King George V who, shortly afterwards on the 7th November 1919, proclaimed by decree:

"Tuesday next, November 11, is the first anniversary of the Armistice, which stayed the worldwide carnage of the four preceding years and the victory of Right and Freedom. I believe that my people in every part

of the Empire fervently wish to perpetuate the meaning of the Great Deliverance, and of those who laid down their lives to achieve it.

To afford an opportunity for the universal expression of their feeling, it is my desire and hope that at the hour when the Armistice comes into force, the eleventh hour of the eleventh day of the eleventh month, there may be for a brief space of two minutes, a complete suspension of all our normal activity ... so that in perfect stillness, the thoughts of everyone may be concentrated on reverent remembrance of the glorious dead."

Sir Percy, when he heard the news that his suggestion had reached the King stated, *"I was so stunned by the news that I could not leave the hotel. An hour or two afterwards I received a cable from Lord Long of Wexhall: "Thank you. Walter Long." Only then did I know that my proposal had reached the King and had been accepted and that the Cabinet knew the source."*

Later, Sir Percy was thanked for his suggestion of the two minute silence by Lord Stamfordham, the King's Private Secretary who wrote:
"Dear Sir Percy,
The King, who learns that you are shortly to leave for South Africa, desires me to assure you that he ever gratefully remembers that the idea of the Two Minute Pause on Armistice Day was due to your initiation, a suggestion readily adopted and carried out with heartfelt sympathy throughout the Empire.
Signed – Stamfordham"

And so the tradition of 2 minutes of silence during remembrance occasions was born through a unique South African gift to the world, a simple peaceful gesture that in deep solitude remembers the end of all war – not the beginning.

By kind permission from Peter Dickens and the South African Military website, The Observation Post - https://samilhistory.com/2016/11/04/2-minutes-silence-a-uniquely-south-african-gift-to-remembrance/